GLIMPSES
OF GOD

GLIMPSES
Stories that Point the Way
OF GOD

SCOTT WALKER

Augsburg
MINNEAPOLIS

To Floyd and Harriett Thatcher

*It is because of your love, encouragement, and support
that I am able to experience the joy of writing.
You are a gift from God.*

GLIMPSES OF GOD
Stories that Point the Way

Unless otherwise noted, scripture quotations are from the New Revised Standard Version Bible, copyright © 1989 by the Division of Christian Education of the National Council of the Churches of Christ in the U.S.A. and used by permission.

Scripture quotations noted GNB are from the *Good News Bible*—Old Testament: copyright © 1976 by the American Bible Society; New Testament—New Testament: copyright © 1966, 1971, 1976 by the American Bible Society. Used by permission.

Scripture quotations noted Phillips are from *The New Testament in Modern English*, copyright © 1958 by J. B. Phillips. Used by permission of the Macmillan Company, New York.

Scripture quotations noted KJV are from the Holy Bible, King James Version.

Cover and book design by Elizabeth Boyce
Cover photo by Michael Melford/Image Bank

ISBN 0-8066-3332-8

The paper used in this publication meets the minimum requirements of American National Standard for Information Sciences—Permanence of Paper for Printed Library Materials, ANSI Z329.48-1984. ∞

Manufactured in the U.S.A.   AF 9-3332

01   00   99   98   97   1   2   3   4   5   6   7   8   9   10

CONTENTS

GLIMPSES OF TIME AND ETERNITY

INTRODUCTION

SOMETIMES THERE IS NO BETTER WAY TO point to truth than to tell a good story—a tale that makes children grow silent and adults sit up and listen. Twenty-eight years ago I encountered a gripping experience that gave me insight into the mystery of God and the nature of life. This primal moment gave birth to the theme of this book—that God often reveals himself to us in sudden, fleeting, and unexpected glimpses. I'd like for you to sit back, relax, and let me tell this story.

Like debtors sprung from prison, my high school buddies and I walked with light frisky steps toward my car. Loose gravel crunched under our heavy hunting boots as we placed our rifles and shells in the trunk. Joyfully we shouted our vapored voices into the chill of a January sky. It was so good to be alive! There was a clear, frozen, crystalline purity to life that could put goose bumps on the dead. To shout and laugh was the only appropriate response to this day of living.

I was shouting for another reason. My drivers license. I had finally gotten it. Turned sixteen! Now I was a man! I could tote a rifle, drive a car, chew tobacco, and go wherever I pleased. I was popping buttons off my hunting vest.

The four of us loaded up and drove off. The afternoon was so vibrant and bright that reading road signs hurt my eyes. Stark, barren pecan trees leaped out against the sky. It would be a great Saturday for squirrel hunting.

8 As I drove down the highway amid jokes and youthful banter, I found myself grinning for another reason. I had a secret. And the secret was that I hated hunting. As a ten year old, I had triumphantly killed a bluejay with a BB gun. Childish excitement had quickly changed to a flood of tears as I buried the slack-necked bird in my mother's garden. On that day I had sworn off killing. Now, I aimed to miss. The boys thought that I was a bad shot. I was better than they knew.

But, then again, I loved hunting. I loved the companionship and the bold "bear stories." The smell of gun oil and pungent cordite was somehow elating. But most of all, I loved the woods. Nothing could be finer than to slither down among the leaves, lean back against the trunk of an oak, and listen to the world grow silent. It was like becoming one with nature. A reunification of heart and soul and mind took place. I felt at home.

Swanson's Woods lay nestled in a river valley. As we crossed the Black Creek bridge, I pulled over to the broad shoulder of the road and parked. To get from the car to the woods we would have to trudge across several broad, fallow fields.

After twenty minutes of stumbling over the dry brittle carcasses of last season's cornstalks and gingerly crossing a half dozen barbed wire fences, we made it to the edge of the woods. Deciding to split up, we agreed to meet back at the edge of the field three hours later at six o'clock. Aware that dusk is often when the woods are most alive, we wanted to squeeze every moment out of the daylight.

As I walked alone deep into the forest, I made mental notes of how to return to our rendezvous. Gradually, I heard my buddies' steps receding. Finally, standing still, I experienced perfect silence. The time had come to find a place to hide and while away the afternoon.

Spying an old walnut tree with thick foliage at its base, I crawled under its encircling brush and fashioned a lair from which to view this woodland world. Convinced that I was camouflaged, I rejoiced in a feeling of womb-like anonymity. All was hushed and still.

Slowly the woods began to return to life. Birds twittered. Leaves crackled as unseen animals scurried about. And in the distance there was the occasional muffled shot of a rifle, a reminder that all was not Eden.

Overcome with a sense of peaceful rest, and burrowing deeper into leaves and flannel to blunt the cold, I shut my eyes and watched shadowed images dance behind my eyelids. With no desire to do so, and yet no will to resist, I fell blissfully to sleep.

Stiff and shaking, I jolted awake. Freezing rain was falling, and it was nearly dark. Frantically I peered through the shadows at my watch and with relief saw that it was 5:45. I had dozed for nearly two hours and now had fifteen minutes to make it back.

Grabbing the shotgun I had never loaded, I ran through the descending dusk. Winter days were so short now. By six o'clock it would be totally dark. With branches tearing at my clothes, I recoiled as a moist spider web brushed across my face. Hurriedly wiping the clinging mess from my nose and forehead, I hoped the spider had seen me coming and abandoned ship. Shuddering, I crashed on through the dimness.

Out of breath, I crested a knoll and reached the open fields. Coasting to a stop, I heard in the distance something unmistakable: the deep rumbling approach of a winter thunderstorm.

The rain pelted down harder, lightning ripping the sky. We had misjudged our time. It was now almost completely dark. Stepping out into the field, I heard their voices before I saw them. Bobby and Tim were fifty yards north of me huddled under a large tree. Relieved, I ran to greet them.

"Where you been, goofball?" Tim chided. "We've been waiting on you an hour!"

"Sure you have!" I shot back, looking around. "Where's Jim?"

"He's not back either," Bobby grumbled. "If he ain't here in five minutes, I vote we leave his no good hide."

Shivering, we stared into the gloom of the forest and listened for the sound of approaching footsteps. Suddenly a muffled shot rang out. It was downfield about a quarter of a mile. Jim was lost and looking for us.

Tim fired a shot into the air, which was immediately answered in the distance. That confirmed it. With Bobby cussing a blue streak, we took off through the darkness, staying in the field but hugging the tree line.

Stumbling blindly across hard frosted furrows, we heard Jim fire his rifle again and again. Finally we could hear him hollering. By the time we found him the luminous dial on my watch reflected 6:30. With thick storm clouds massed overhead, it was now pitch black.

Too tired to give Jim a hard time, we huddled together as cold rain drenched us. In our haste to find Jim, we had become completely disoriented.

"Where's the car, man?" Bobby asked me.

"Back to the left somewhere," I replied, staring into the darkness.

"It must be a mile away," Tim grumbled as he began to move back to the west. "Let's go!"

Slowly picking our way back along the tree line, I could hear a creek begin to gurgle as torrential rain increased its flow. The storm was quickly becoming vicious.

Suddenly a blaze of lightning turned night into day and thunder shook the ground. Nearly blinded, I thought I saw a metallic glint in the distance on the other side of the field. Maybe it was the car. But now all I could see was a glaring green spot throbbing against the darkness.

"Wait, you guys!" I hollered. "I think I saw the car! Wait till the lightning flashes again."

For nearly a minute we stood still, breathing hard and staring tensely into the darkness. When the lightning spread across the sky, we clung to every glimmer of light. In one ecstatic voice we shouted as four pairs of eyes became riveted on the dim outline of the car a quarter mile away. Fixing the position firmly in our minds, we began to move across open field as darkness covered us again.

Without agreeing to do so, I noticed that we were all slowing our pace, hanging back, waiting expectantly. Adapting to the darkness, we each had learned to walk fifty yards and pause for the next glimpse of light to pierce the night.

Suddenly the lightning exploded again, and I could see that there was only one more fence to cross. With relief we slogged across a final muddy gully and groped our way up the ditch along the side of the road. Ice was forming on the side of the car; it shattered and fell as we jerked open the doors.

Huddled inside, nobody said a word. We were too frozen to move. Again the lightning flashed and we could see the white highway lines disappear into darkness. Only then did I turn on the headlights and place the key in the ignition. The engine roared to life, and four soaked and sheepish boys headed home.

It has been a long time since I experienced that turbulent night. But I have not forgotten some important lessons I learned.

Perhaps, above all, the graphic imagery of the lightning has seared across my memory. As we stood in stormy darkness, only the periodic flashes of lightning gave my friends and me brief glimpses into where we were and where our future steps must go. The lightning was a pure gift; nothing we had earned or could make happen. With all of our frantic willpower we could not generate nor coerce its bursts of illumination. Rather, the lightning came to us. It was something that graced our path and gave to us a sense of direction in the midst of our wandering and perplexity.

Many times since that night I have again experienced life as one who is lost and in need of insight and guidance. Even in the brilliance of noonday, my internal world has sometimes been shrouded and obscure, and I have found myself fighting panic and confusion. Perhaps I have been perplexed about what my future holds or what vocational path I should take. At other

12 times I have been lacking in wisdom as to how to approach a problem or groping in the dark as to where a solution might be found. In all of these moments of lostness, blindness, and insecurity, I have found that God has been faithful to send the lightning again—a flash of something that gave me a momentary glimpse into my future or the meaning of my life.

Often these glimpses have come in the simplest and gentlest of ways. Rarely do they have the brilliant and burning character of lightning or the jarring power of thunder. These glimpses are frequently found in common everyday occurrences: the stories of a friend, the reverie of a midnight stroll, the innocent question of a child, a poignant memory, a daydream during church, a good belly laugh, or the words on a printed page. Yet, whenever the lightning arcs again and a glimpse is seen, I find, in the words of C.S. Lewis, that I am "surprised by joy."

Why joy? Well, it is the delightful discovery that I am not so lost after all. It is the unexpected reassurance that God is with me and is faithful to give me the necessary guidance to take the next small step in my life. It is the sudden flash of God's smile, the roar of his laughter, the power of his presence. It is an awareness of the spark of a fragile holy moment; a flame that will flare and dim. These brief glimpses of insight bring with them great joy and reassurance.

This book is a collage of such glimpses, a collection of stories that have revealed to me the nature of God and secrets of life. Many of these insights have come as gifts and surprises from others who have never known they were gift-givers, because none of us truly know when God's lightning flashes through us and brightens the darkness of another.

I share these glimpses with you with the prayer that they will spark your own memory and you will see how God has revealed his way to you. Lets walk together for awhile and share a few stories along the way.

The crash of your thunder was in the whirlwind;
The lightnings lit up the world;
The earth trembled and shook.
You led your people like a flock
by the hand of Moses and Aaron.
    PSALM 77:18-20

The Lord went in front of them in a pillar of cloud by day,
to lead them along the way, and in a pillar of fire by night,
to give them light, so that they might travel by day and by
night. Neither the pillar of cloud by day nor the pillar of
fire by night left its place in front of the people.
    EXODUS 13:21-22

When he utters his voice, there is a tumult of waters
    in the heavens,
and he makes the mist rise from the ends of the earth.
He makes lightning for the rain,
and he brings out the wind from his storehouses.
Everyone is stupid and without knowledge;
Not like these is the Lord, the portion of Jacob,
for he is the one who formed all things,
and Israel is the tribe of his inheritance;
the Lord of hosts is his name.
    JEREMIAH 51:16-17A, 19

A glimpse is not a vision. But to a man on a mountain
road by night, a glimpse of the next three feet of road may
matter more than a vision of the horizon.[1]
    C. S. LEWIS

14   *God often gives in one brief moment that which he has for*
       a long time denied.[2]
      THOMAS À KEMPIS

Journey by Night

Thou who never canst err, for Thyself are the Way;
Thou whose infinite kingdom is flooded with day;
Thou whose eyes behold all, for Thyself art the light,
Look down on us gently who journey by night.

By the pity reveled in Thy loneliest hour,
Forsaken, self-bound and self-emptied of power;
Thou who, even in death, hadst all heaven in sight,
Look down on us gently who journey by night.

On the road to Emmaus, they thought Thou wast dead;
Yet they saw Thee and knew Thee in the breaking of bread.
Though the day was spent, in Thy face there was light.
Look down on us gently who journey by night.[3]
      ALFRED NOYES

Creator God, we all journey by night. We cannot see our hand before our face unless you give us light and vision. Our greatest fear is that we walk alone, lost on a journey without purpose or direction.

O God, may your lightning flash and illumine our path to traverse this day. May we be content to take one step at a time.

Grant that the pages of this book will be used by your Spirit to give glimpses of truth. And may stories shared together lend companionship to all who walk alone.

I pray this in the name of one who also walked in darkness but is the light of the world, Jesus Christ, my Lord. Amen.

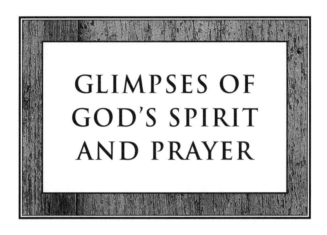

GLIMPSES OF GOD'S SPIRIT AND PRAYER

THE POWER
OF THE UNIVERSE

IT WAS HARD TO BELIEVE THAT THEY
had once been young, as young as I when I first met them. I was
an impetuous redheaded kid. They were tall and silver-haired,
with thin, angular features carved by time.

Mr. and Mrs. Herold were our neighbors. We were all dis-
located Americans living high in the rugged Benguet mountains on the northern island of Luzon in the Philippine
Islands. Less than a year before, my family had come as missionaries. The Herolds had lived on this sharp mountain range
for decades.

They had arrived shortly after the turn of the twentieth century. America had just defeated Spain in the Spanish-American
War. As an unexpected consequence, the Spanish territory of the
Philippines had become an American protectorate. With typical
colonial conquer-the-world naivete, the United States govern-
ment quickly recruited hundreds of young American college
graduates and sent them to the Philippines as teachers. They
were to infiltrate the "boondocks" and bring literacy, hygiene,
and Western knowledge to the Filipinos. The Herolds were some
of those bright-eyed American young people who had walked
ashore so many years ago.

Now, fifty years later, they owned a thriving lumber company in the city of Baguio in Mountain Province. But progress
and prosperity had not come easily. As a young boy, I loved to
hear the Herolds reflect on the struggles of their pioneering days.

18   One story I have never forgotten involved the building of the first road to Baguio.

When the Herolds were first assigned to teach in Mountain Province, the steep ridges that towered a mile above sea level could not be traversed by road or rail. The only transportation was by horseback over treacherous trading paths. Though highly skilled and intelligent, the rugged Igorot tribesmen they were to teach were totally unexposed to Western culture or modern technology. These strong and fierce people were best known for head-hunting and for building ingenious systems of terraced and self-irrigating rice paddies. Few had seen automobiles, and none had built roads.

Though a teacher, Mr. Herold had also studied engineering. When the time came to build a road high into the mountains, he volunteered his services.

The task was awesome. The mountain range had been formed by violent volcanic activity. The mountains jutted straight out of the ocean and towered into the sky. You could stand on the mile-high peaks and clearly see the South China Sea only twenty miles away. In building any road to Baguio there would be steep inclines to traverse and powerful rivers to span.

What made the task most difficult was the lack of modern machinery. Dynamite could be obtained, but there was no earth-moving equipment. Tons of dirt and boulders had to be moved by pick and shovel and human strength.

Progress moved at a snail's pace. The muscular Igorot tribesmen worked hard and diligently. Scantily dressed in g-strings, these short, fierce warriors seemed to be tireless. And the raven-haired Igorot women, topless and clad only in brightly woven skirts, worked right beside the men. With their mouths and teeth stained red and orange from chewing betel nut, and their brown tattooed bodies glistening with sweat, the Igorots bravely attacked the mountainside.

One day Mr. Herold rode his horse down the mountain trail to a port city to buy supplies. While purchasing dynamite and other supplies from the docks, he uncovered a crate filled with bright, shiny wheelbarrows from the United States. Not believing his good fortune, he quickly bought them, loaded them on an old borrowed truck, and hastily bumped and banged his way up the rutted new roadbed as night descended.

The next day as Mr. Herold left the engineer's base camp with the new wheelbarrows and headed toward the work site, he was in a terrific hurry. He had promised to return the borrowed truck to the docks by noon but had overslept. Now he would be hours late.

Slinging rocks and gravel as he careened into the construction site, Mr. Herold quickly unloaded the wheelbarrows. He hastily instructed the Igorot foreman to guard these novelties so they would not be stolen, and immediately jumped back into the truck and bounced back down the road.

It was three days before Mr. Herold was able to return to the work site. And when he did, he almost fell off of his horse with laughter. There before him were the dozen new wheelbarrows safe and sound. In fact, they were not only safe, the Igorots were already energetically and enthusiastically using them.

Having never seen a wheelbarrow, the Igorot foreman had assigned four men to each wheelbarrow. With shovels they would quickly fill the wheelbarrows to the rim with rock and dirt. Then the four men would each grab a corner of the wheelbarrow, grimace as they lifted it, then grunt and groan as they carried it on their shoulders to a ravine where the dirt was dumped. For them, a wheelbarrow was simply a large metal container to carry. The wheel was useless.

Why have I remembered this story when a thousand others have passed into the oblivion of faded memory? Perhaps even as a boy I sensed that this pioneer's story was a glimpse into a basic truth of life, a truth on which I have reflected many times.

There is so much power in this universe that has never been tapped. For eons human beings lived without knowing the might and utility of the wheel. They struggled to transport boulders to

20   build walls, move logs from deep forests, and carry heavy produce to market. Their only help was the strong back of oxen and
other domesticated animals. Then, over 6,000 years ago, the
Sumerians in the Tigris-Euphrates Valley invented the wheel and
fashioned crude carts and wagons. Suddenly, human history was
radically changed.

Centuries passed and new sources of power were discovered:
wind, water, steam, coal, electricity, nuclear energy, and now
solar energy. I have to believe that our universe is simply filled
with sources of vitality that we have not yet discovered, much
less applied.

The human brain is such an under-utilized source of power.
Doctors and scientists tell us that only a small portion of our
brain's capability is used. What would happen if we were to discover ways to unleash all of the potential of the human mind?
Perhaps such science-fiction scenarios as mental telepathy and
physical levitation might not be so farfetched after all.

If this is true of the physical world, it is also true of the spiritual world. Jesus of Nazareth had access to sources of spiritual
power that few of us have experienced. He spoke to his disciples
about this power during his final days on earth. Knowing that
they would struggle to cope with the intense pressure and challenge of future days, Jesus promised to give them an increased
source of spiritual power. He said to them, "But you will receive
power when the Holy Spirit has come upon you" (Acts 1:8). At
another time he promised, "And I will ask the Father, and he will
give you another Advocate, to be with you forever"(John 14:16).
We know this source of power and help that Jesus referred to as
the Holy Spirit.

Later, the apostle Paul was to experience the strength of the
Holy Spirit, just as Jesus promised. Writing to the church in Eph-
esus, Paul gives insight into the nature of the Holy Spirit. He
states, "How very great is his power at work in us who believe.
This power working in us is the same as the mighty strength he
used when he raised Christ from death (Eph. 1:19-20, GNB).

Paul clearly states that the same spiritual power that raised Jesus from the dead is available for you and me to experience today. This spiritual power emanates from God—indeed, is God—and we can have access to God's power if we so desire.

However, I often find myself in the same plight as the Igorot tribesmen with the wheelbarrow. I want to fill my life to the brim with the weight and responsibility of my world and then carry it all on my shoulders. Too often I have been unaware that the Spirit of God is there to help me. It is a discovery I have been slow to make.

Looking back over my life from the vantage point of middle age, I can see that my understanding of God has come in stages. For the first twenty years of my life, my Christian faith and experience were more of a family tradition than anything else. Born into a Christian family, I was taught the basic doctrines of Christianity from childhood. I went to church with the same regularity and unquestioning compliance as I went to school. I was simultaneously a Walker, an American, and a Christian because I had been born that way. This was my tradition, my heritage of faith.

Somewhere in my late teens and early twenties, a revolution of thought and perspective began to take place in my life. Like most young adults, I began to seriously question the "faith of my fathers." I realized that if I were going to believe in God, my belief had to be based on something more than family tradition and cultural conditioning. And so I launched into an intense, frightening, and exhilarating experience of "finding God" for myself.

Over the last twenty years, I have spent much time and effort establishing my own basis for Christian faith. Today I have developed a theology and an intellectual framework that is truly my own. My faith is more than tradition. Now it is my own discovery, an authentic part of who I am. To a great extent, I know what I believe and why I believe it.

However, in recent months, I have seen a whole new chapter in my pilgrimage of faith emerging. As the total weight of

22   adulthood has been placed on my weary shoulders, I have come
to see that belief in God is not enough. In addition to intellectual
understanding and assent, I also need an *experience* of the power
and the presence of God. I have filled my wheelbarrow full of
weighty thoughts, but now I need to discover a spiritual wheel.

Something about the adult years—the challenges of marriage, the responsibility of parenthood, the ever-increasing
demands of vocation, the creeping awareness of mortality,
wrestling with your dreams, the intoxication of success, the fear
of failure, a hunger for God—causes us to reach out for strength
and power beyond ourself. Only then are we ready to discover
the Holy Spirit of God, the wheel of the universe on which all
else revolves.

The promise of Jesus is clear. There is a Power, a Spirit, a
Helper, that is with us all the time. It is crucial that we discover
and utilize this power if the road to our future is to ever be completed and the mountaintops of our world reached.

Then afterward
I will pour out my spirit on all flesh;
your sons and your daughters shall prophesy,
your old men shall dream dreams,
and your young men shall see visions.
    JOEL 2:28

And I will ask the Father, and he will give you another
Advocate, to be with you forever. This is the Spirit of truth,
whom the world cannot receive, because it neither sees him
nor knows him. You know him because he abides with you,
and he will be in you. I will not leave you orphaned; I am
coming to you.
    JOHN 14:16-18

But you will receive power when the Holy Spirit has come upon you; and you will be my witnesses both in Jerusalem, in all Judea and Samaria, and to the ends of the earth.
ACTS 1:8

The early church was Spirit-centered. Its ethic was an ethic of the Holy Spirit. As time passed, the Spirit became peripheral and secondary in the life of the church. Toward the end of the first century, the Logos doctrine tended to supplant the Spirit as the life force of the churches. By the time of the Middle Ages the Logos had become a metaphysical principle rather than a living personal Lord whose work was made effective by the Spirit. Today, organized effort, rather that the power of the Spirit, has tended to become the pattern of the church. The Spirit has been retained as a doctrine without being effective in Christian experience.[1]
HENLEE H. BARNETTE

It is easy to sit in discussion groups, to sit in a study and to read books, it is easy to discuss the intellectual truth of Christianity; but the essential thing is to experience the power of Christianity. And it is fatally easy to start at the wrong end and to think of Christianity as something to be discussed, not as something to be experienced. It is certainly important to have an intellectual grasp of the orb of Christian truth; but it is still more important to have a vital experience of the power of Jesus Christ.[2]
WILLIAM BARCLAY

Without the power of the Holy Spirit all human efforts, methods, and plans are as futile as attempting to propel a boat by puffing at the sails with our own breath.[3]
D. M. DAWSON

Christianity does not consist in abstaining from doing things no gentleman would think of doing, but in doing things that are unlikely to occur to anyone who is not in touch with the Spirit of Christ.[4]

R. H. L. SHEPPARD

Dear Lord, all my life I have been trying to move mountains, to build roads that have no end. I am tired. My wheelbarrow has grown too heavy. I cannot lift it alone.

Teach me to use the wheel of your Spirit. With your help, may I discover that your load is easy and your burden is light. May I come to believe and experience the Helper that you promised. Amen.

WIRE AND TINFOIL

2

SATURDAY HAD BEEN ONE OF THOSE days. It was supposed to be my day off and wasn't. I was dragging home dog tired when I looked up and saw my mother's car parked in our driveway. Now, I love my mother, but on this particular afternoon there was one thing that I did not want and that was unexpected company. Groaning out loud, I slid into my martyr complex and opened the front door.

Our children were wild! Drew greeted me sliding down the stair rail; a forbidden delight. Jodi was screaming while Luke prodded and teased her. My mother stood in the middle of the living room like a veteran traffic cop trying desperately to gain control of a gyrating situation. Suddenly, I was glad she was there.

As I greeted Mom and bent to kiss her cheek, she whispered, "I hope you remembered today is Valentine's Day!" I groaned again for the tenth time in the last minute. "Remembered! I haven't even thought about it!"

Beating a hasty retreat to the door, I knew I could rush to the corner store and at least buy a box of candy to temporarily plug the hole in the dike. That's when my wife Beth intercepted me and blocked my escape.

"Scott, I need you to drive to the Redd's with me and load their portable crib in my car. It's too heavy for me to lift."

There was no use arguing, so I dutifully followed her to the car. She pulled out her keys and slid into the driver's seat. "Well, at least I'm going to be chauffeured!" I muttered to myself.

26   At the end of our street, Beth took a left when she should have turned right. "The Redd's is that way!" I growled and gestured.

"I know that, grouch!" she shot back. "There's someplace else we need to go first."

"Great!" I thought. "Five more minutes, and the store closes." I gave up and settled in for a long evening.

As block after block flashed by and we neared the outskirts of town, I sat in sulky silence, deep within my own thoughts. The last months had been difficult ones. Hurricane Hugo had torn through our community of Charleston, South Carolina, and demolished our church's sanctuary. Now, nearly two years later, we were finishing our restoration project and had just concluded our fund drive. I was worn out with the long and constant pressures of crisis. I was not my old jovial self.

"Where are you going?" I finally asked.

"What do you mean *you*, big fella! I think you mean where are *we* going," Beth shot back with an impish smile.

"All right. Enough's enough! We just left the city limits. Where are *we* going?"

Pointing to the back seat, she said, "Why don't you look under those blankets."

As I glanced over my shoulder, I saw a rectangular object covered by a plaid blanket. Tossing back the blanket, I found my suitcase and a suit bag. Stunned, I growled, "Beth! What in the world is going on?"

Beth exploded in childish delight. "I've always wanted to go to Beaufort by the sea," she laughed. "And we're going! Going right now! Happy Valentine's Day!"

Totally flustered, I blurted, "Honey, we've got church tomorrow! I've gotta preach. What in the world are you thinking about?"

"I've thought about everything, hot shot. Russel is preaching for you tomorrow. I asked him three weeks ago. And your Mom's keeping the kids. We've got a beautiful room at a bed and breakfast overlooking the bay. It has a double bed, a shower, even a TV for your ball game. Just be quiet and enjoy the ride. I'm in control of this one."

As the beauty of Beth's surprise slowly sank in, I felt tears sting my eyes and a silly grin stretch across my face. I felt like a slave granted his freedom. I began to do something I hadn't done in weeks, laugh uncontrollably. Beth had given me more than a present. She had given me an unexpected spark of life. It was an incredible gift for both of us.

Two days later, I felt like a new man. Rested and refreshed, I found my life suddenly rich and full of color again. After a wonderful dinner on our final night in Beaufort, I walked across our room to the TV and for the first time flicked it on. Duke was playing North Carolina, and it was billed as the game of the year. What a way to spend an evening!

Much to my dismay, no picture emerged on the screen. Murky figures swirled into each other, and the announcer's muffled voice was faint. Obviously there was a reception problem. Running downstairs to talk to the innkeeper, I discovered that a storm had recently blown down the antenna. The television was out of commission until repairs were made.

Disappointed, I trudged back upstairs. A Duke fan, I really wanted to see the game. With a burst of determination, I decided that I was not going to give up so easily.

Grabbing my toolbox from the car, I asked the innkeeper for some tin foil. With coat hangers from the closet, I fashioned a makeshift antenna from the foil and wire and connected it to the television. Much to my surprise, the picture suddenly sprang into focus, and the announcer's voice became crystal clear. Never known for my mechanical skills, I felt a strange surge of manly pride. I had fixed the sucker—and Duke won the game!

That surprise weekend has filled my life with wonderful memories. It also gave me meaningful visual images with which to remember some important spiritual truths.

28   All of us have our down times. Due to fatigue, stress, crises, and hectic schedules, we often find ourselves depressed and despondent. Joy in life and the revitalizing Spirit of God seem a million miles away. We can't get on top of our physical and spiritual malaise.

In a way, we are like the television set without an antenna. Just as television waves filled the room that night, so the Spirit of God always surrounds us, infiltrating our total being. Yet, for some reason, we are unable to tune in and receive God's strength, peace, joy, and vitality. Our picture of the world remains murky, and our perspective of reality becomes distorted. God's voice is muffled. How can we change our situation, be empowered by God's Spirit, and return to spiritual health? How can we fashion our own spiritual antenna and get back in touch with God?

Perhaps the first step is to do what Beth forced me to do: to get away from it all, goof off, take a retreat, remove ourselves from crisis, and spend some time in relaxed solitude. This is exactly what Jesus did. Perhaps Jesus never went to a lovely bed and breakfast by the sea, but the Gospel writers tell us that during pivotal moments of crisis he always went on retreat.

The first retreat that Jesus took occurred at the beginning of his ministry. He had just been baptized by John the Baptist. Now his public ministry loomed before him. How was he to tell his people about the nature and love of God? Was he to immediately go to Jerusalem and make a dramatic and public spectacle of himself? Was he to imitate John the Baptist and become a stern and eccentric "voice crying in the wilderness"? Was he to raise an army and declare himself the heir to the throne of David? Overcome by such a quandary, he withdrew to a place of solitude in the desert to meditate, ponder, and pray. Slowly, his way became clear to him (Matthew 4:1-11).

Later, in the middle of Jesus' ministry, he encountered another crisis when after miraculously feeding the hungry crowds, they wanted "to come and take him by force, to make him king" (John 6:15). Even his twelve disciples appeared to be sympathetic with the demands of the enthralled crowds. What did Jesus do? He dispersed the frenetic mob, made the disciples get into their boat and sail away, and then Jesus "went up on the mountain to pray" (Mark 6:45-46; John 6:1-15). Only after removing himself from the stress and demands of so many people could Jesus then be able to return to his disciples, walking confidently on the deep waters.

Finally, in the waning hours of Jesus' life, when it seemed that his whole world was crashing down on him and death was inescapable, he again went on retreat. Taking with him only his disciples, he slipped into a private room in a secluded home to enjoy a special meal and a night of fellowship. Later they went to a favorite "getaway place" of Jesus—a quiet hillside garden called Gethsemane. There, knowing that he faced imminent arrest, he said to his disciples, "Keep awake and pray that you may not come into temptation; the spirit indeed is willing, but the flesh is weak" (Mark 14:38).

Jesus knew that without such retreat, none of them could get through the next few hours. This revitalizing time prepared Jesus to walk into the certain jaws of death and not beat a hasty retreat to Galilee. Without this time to regroup and regain depleted strength, Jesus could well have crumpled under the vicious trial and torture of the Jews and Romans. Yet because Jesus took seriously the importance of spiritual and physical retreat, he was able to persevere through the dreaded physical abuse and an agonizing death. For the Christian there must be quiet before the storm because "the spirit indeed is willing, but the flesh is weak."

Beth and I have both learned that in our lives and marriage we must spend time alone. At least twice a year I go off by myself for several days. Many times good friends let me use their beach house for a hideaway. There I write, read, meditate, pray, sleep, run, take long walks, and do the things that revitalize my life and spirit. I have come to love this time alone.

At first, Beth thought that my need for solitude was a little strange and threatening. It seemed to imply that my need to get

30 away meant that there was something wrong with her, that she and the children could not meet my needs, that I did not need them. However, now that she has also gone away for some days by herself, she has discovered that retreat and solitude can indeed strengthen family relationships, because it restores our energy and desire to relate lovingly to each other.

As the great spiritual mystics have always known, solitude and quietness are God's food for the soul. In our busy and hectic world, we must create for ourselves times of retreat and quiet contemplation.

However, solitude by itself is not enough to put us into contact with God's Spirit. In the midst of solitude we can get lost and swallowed up unless we also pray. After all, in the quiet stillness of Gethsemane, the disciples simply fell asleep. It was Jesus who came to them and said, "Are you asleep? Could you not keep awake one hour? Keep awake and pray that you may not come into temptation"(Mark 14:37-38).

Prayer is like the antenna on the television. A room can be literally saturated with television waves. However unless the television in that room has an antenna, a picture cannot be received and a voice heard. Likewise, we can be alone and surrounded by God's Spirit, but without the spiritual antenna of prayer, it is difficult to gain a clear perspective of our lives, to clearly perceive God's will and to hear his voice.

Unfortunately, many Christians have a limited view of prayer. We feel that prayer takes place only when we *talk* to God, when we put our thoughts and feelings into words and tell God what is on our minds. Though this form of prayer is important and indispensable, it is only one variation on a theme, one golf club within a whole bag of clubs, one color on an artist's palette. There are many other ways to pray.

My own approaches to prayer come in many forms. I love to run. Indeed running has become for me a catalyst for prayer, a way in which I meet God in this world. Somehow running releases my deep subconscious thoughts. As the miles flash by, I find my thoughts percolating and being directed in a thousand different ways. Yet after thirty minutes of hard breathing and working up a good sweat, I find that many of my scattered thoughts begin to fall into place; I encounter some of my most creative insights; I discover that I am listening to God and he is speaking to me. Indeed, most of my sermons and book chapters are conceived while I am running.

Exercise—whether it be running, walking, swimming, biking, canoeing, or golfing—can be a way of communicating with God. As we fill our expanding lungs deeply with the breathe of life and murmur our thoughts to God, God revitalizes our spiritual fatigue with the energizing presence of his spirit.

I have also discovered that quiet, non-verbal meditation is a powerful form of prayer. Growing up in southeast Asia, I remember as a boy watching saffron-robed Buddhist monks sitting in the lotus position for hours in total silence. At the time I thought that they were simply weird. Now, as an adult, I know that they had discovered something important.

My first experience with meditation came during seminary days. Most of my professors would begin their classes with prayer. Some would read a prayer from one of the devotional classics. Others would speak to God in their own words. Occasionally a professor would make sure that his students were awake by suddenly calling on one of us to pray. It always worked.

My pastoral counseling professor, Dr. Edward Thornton, approached his classes differently. A very spiritual person, he had discovered the power of meditation through the struggles of his own life and he wanted to impart this secret to his students. So, on the first day of class, rather than beginning with spoken prayer, he began to teach us some of the simple techniques of quiet meditation.

At first, most of us thought that Dr. Thornton had lost his marbles. Indeed, a few narrow-minded students refused to participate and dropped his class. But quietly he taught us how

32   to sit up straight, how to breathe and exhale in a slow rhythmic pattern, and how to simply let our thoughts drift and the presence of God slowly permeate our being. Each day for five minutes we would begin class with silent meditation and it made a lasting difference in my life.

Through a psalm writer God said, "Be still, and know that I am God"(Psalm 46:10). Meditation is a way that we can discipline ourselves to sit, be quiet, and listen to the Spirit of God.

In order to pray we don't have to get on our knees and put into words all of our thoughts and feelings. There are other forms of wire and tin foil by which to fashion an antenna. In the midst of our spiritual solitude we can run and play; we can sit, meditate, even drive a car; we can write, read, or spontaneously speak our thoughts to God; for it is all the same, all different forms of one essential thing called prayer.

Most of us are assaulted with far more stress in the routine of life than we can handle alone. We need periodically to get away, to retreat to solitude, to extend our spiritual antennae and grow reconnected to the Spirit of God. Sometimes it takes the encouragement of somebody else to convince us to do it. A few of us knuckleheads even have to be kidnapped and forcibly whisked away. So, don't wait too long. Do something good for yourself. Spend a few hours—a few days—in solitude with God.

Those of steadfast mind you keep in peace—in peace because they trust in you.
    ISAIAH 26:3

But whenever you pray, go into your room and shut the door and pray to your Father who is in secret, and your Father who sees in secret will reward you.
    MATTHEW 6:6-7

Jesus, full of the Holy Spirit, returned from the Jordan and was led by the Spirit in the wilderness. . . . Then Jesus, filled with the power of the Spirit, returned to Galilee.
LUKE 4:1, 14

Our language has wisely sensed the two sides of being alone. It has created the word "loneliness" to express the pain of being alone. And it has created the word "solitude" to express the glory of being alone.[1]
PAUL TILLICH

When the conflicting currents of the unconscious create engulfing whirlpools, the waters can again be guided into a single current if the dam sluice be opened into the channel of prayer—and if that channel has been dug deep enough.[2]
DAG HAMMARSKJÖLD

Prayer is not instinctive like eating. I wish it were, and that one really hungered for God. If I give up food, I am driven to eat; the less I eat the more I want to, but the less I pray the less I want to.[3]
LESLIE D. WEATHERHEAD

Do not always scrupulously confine yourself to certain rules, or particular forms of devotion, but act with a general confidence in God, with love and humility.[4]
BROTHER LAWRENCE

So sometimes comes to soul and sense
The feeling which is evidence
That very near about us lies
The realm of spiritual mysteries.
The sphere of the supernal powers
Impinges on this world of ours.[5]
JOHN GREENLEAF WHITTIER

Dear God, my calendar is full. I cannot possibly get away for a day or two and spend time with you. Yet, if I don't, I have little to offer to anyone who needs me. I cannot give food from an empty pantry.

Help me to see, O God, that time spent with you is the secret to all love and to all success. If there is not solitude, there can be no service. And if there is not prayer, there can be no love.

May I take my calendar and reserve a day for you. Give me the courage of discipline. Amen.

BRUISED KNUCKLES

3

MY FAMILY AND I LIVED IN THE WON-
derful city of Charleston, South Carolina, for seven years. An
old English colonial town, it is known for its beautiful restored
eighteenth and nineteenth-century homes and lovely gardens.
Crisscrossed by ancient cobblestone streets and narrow walled
alleys, Charleston allows us to step back into time. Nestled by
the Atlantic Ocean, Charleston has a charm like no other city I
have known.

My family and I had the unique opportunity to live in an aged
parsonage, a quaint and beautiful Charleston "single house" built
in 1760. Designed by a sea captain, the old house has survived
numerous hurricanes and earthquakes, the Revolutionary War,
and the intense bombardments of the Civil War. Many nights I
stood on the parsonage's long piazza, staring at a Carolina moon
above the glistening harbor, and wondering how many families
had lived under the roof of this venerable structure.

The seven years in Charleston flew by. Our daughter, Jodi,
was born under the watchcare of the old parsonage. Our sons,
Drew and Luke, grew from toddlers to romping, stomping
healthy boys. Beth and I sank down roots, too. We made many
good friends and established relationships that will span a life-
time. We could have stayed in Charleston for the rest of our lives.
But a restlessness began to grow within me.

Most of us feel restless from time to time. It's not that we are
unhappy or dissatisfied or that we have run out of challenge, but

an intuition begins to grow within us that we are moving toward transition, toward a new chapter in life. It is like the first vague awareness of a fluttering breeze that will slowly grow to fill our sails and propel us along on a different voyage to yet another harbor, another town, another community with its own ways.

Yet "restlessness" means more than that. It means many long nights of lying awake staring at the ceiling and wondering what the future holds. It means impatience: frustration that things are not moving faster, that God is not speaking clearer, that events beyond my control are not going my way or following my schedule. It means fearing that being "restless" is synonymous with being immature, or unappreciative, or being a listless, rootless, tumbleweed blown along by any dusty wind. Going through a restless stage of life is not easy.

Usually when I get restless, I pray a lot—or to be more precise—groan and moan a lot. I want God to get on with the task of leading me.

On one such day of moaning and groaning, I was walking with my boys to a nearby park to play basketball. To get to the park we had to walk down Stoll's Alley, a dark and narrow passageway one hundred yards long, six feet wide, with high brick walls on either side.

Squeezing down the cavernous alley, we were passing a section of wall that protected and shielded a beautiful garden on the other side. The wall was ten feet high, its upper crust studded with shards of jagged, broken glass embedded into cement. No thief would scale this wall.

In the middle of the wall, a shallow alcove housed an imposing wooden door hung on primitive iron hinges. I stared at the oak door shrouded with cobwebs wondering how many years it had been since the large, thick timbers had swiveled on their hinges allowing entrance into the hidden world beyond. For some reason my thoughts flashed to Holman Hunt's painting, "The Light of the World," which depicts Jesus standing by a closed door and knocking.

I stopped as my little boys continued on, lost in their own banter and play. It seemed as if this tall, sturdy door had spontaneously become a symbol for me. It reminded me of my restlessness, my inability to open doors, my lostness in a side alley when I sensed my future lay on the other side of an impenetrable wall.

Staring at the weathered door, I remembered Jesus' words: "Ask and it shall be given; seek, and ye shall find; knock, and it shall be opened unto you." Smiling, I balled my hand into a fist and knocked as loud as I could. Then I ran, catching up with my boys, afraid that somebody really might open that door and find me looking foolish and speechless.

Symbols and rituals in our life start as simply and impulsively as this story. From that day forward, whenever I passed the garden door in Stoll's Alley, I would stop and pound away. If alone I would bow my head and pray, "Lord, in your own good time, open the door and lead me on." Sometimes I would knock angrily, demanding immediate entrance. On good days I would knock with patience, not feeling hurried. On more than one dark night, I rapped with fear and anxiety. I kept on knocking. And knocking. And knocking.

One afternoon, again on the way to the park, my boys saw me stop and knock. Luke looked at me as if I had lost my mind and said, "Daddy, what are you doing?"

Caught in the act, I felt foolish and blurted out, "I'm knocking on God's door."

"What do you mean you're knocking on God's door? God don't live there," Luke replied.

"I know he doesn't, but the Bible tells us that sometimes when we pray we should imagine that we are knocking on a door, asking somebody to open it and let us in. So, sometimes when I'm thinking about God, I just knock on this big old door for fun."

Luke looked at me again as if waiting for the punch line, then flashed his big grin and ran off after his brother, Drew.

38 I forgot about this little transaction until a couple weeks later when we were again traipsing down the alley. I looked up and saw Luke pounding away on the old garden door.

"What are you doing, son?" I asked.

"Thinking about God," he said.

I laughed. Laughed a belly laugh, delighted that the power of symbol had struck home.

Well, I waited for eighteen more months. I almost punched a hole through that door. But the door finally opened. I discovered that on the other side of that Charleston wall was not a garden at all but the vast and panoramic expanse of Texas.

As with the Hebrew children of old wandering and grumbling in the Sinai desert, I have slowly come to see that waiting for the door to be opened is an important time of preparation for the future. God uses restlessness, pain, fear, and frustration to plow the soil of our souls and prepare us for his future place. He uses the long process of knocking to allow hard gained wisdom to slowly seep down into the inner reservoirs of our life. God doesn't open doors until he is ready and we are ready. And, on the other side, there is always surprise.

Yet, God has promised to those who are faithful to knock that he will always open the door. It just requires patience, time, persistence, and bruised knuckles.

Trust in the Lord, and do good;
so you will live in the land, and enjoy security.
Take delight in the Lord;
and he will give you the desires of your heart.
Commit your way to the Lord;
trust in him, and he will act.
Be still before the Lord and wait patiently for him.
    PSALM 37:3-5, 7

But those who wait for the Lord
shall renew their strength,
they shall mount up with wings like eagles,
they shall run and not be weary,
they shall walk and not faint.
    ISAIAH 40:31

Rejoice always, pray without ceasing, give thanks in all
circumstances; for this is the will of God in Christ Jesus
for you.
    1 THESSALONIANS 5:16-18

The fruit of the Spirit is . . . patience.
    GALATIANS 5:22

Rejoice in hope, be patient in suffering, persevere in prayer.
    ROMANS 12:12

God does not always come to us when we want him to. But,
God is always on time.[1]
    J. W. FANNING

Prayer is not an easy way of getting what we want, but the
only way of becoming what God wants us to be.[2]
    ANONYMOUS

On His Blindness

When I consider how my light is spent,
Ere half my days, in this dark world and wide,
And that one talent which is death to hide
Lodged with me useless, though my soul more bent
To serve therewith my Maker, and present
My true account, lest he returning chide,
"Doth God exact day-labour, light denied?"

40

I fondly ask. But Patience, to prevent
That murmur, soon replies: "God doth not need
Either man's work or his own gifts; who best
Bear his mild yoke, they serve him best. His state
Is kingly; thousands at his bidding speed,
And post o'er land and ocean without rest;
They also serve who only stand and wait." [3]
    JOHN MILTON

Dear Lord, so much of life is spent in waiting. Waiting and knocking on closed doors. "What a waste of precious time!" I shout at the heavens. There are better things to do.

Calm me down, Lord. Help me to see that you know the right moment. The right place. I am not squandering time because you are preparing me, shaping me, training me for what lies ahead.

Accept my bruised knuckles as a symbol that I love you. May I trust that you have heard the beating of my heart long before the knocking of my hand. Amen.

FROM THE FAR SIDE OF ETERNITY

IT'S CHRISTMAS TIME AND EXCITEMENT is mounting. Even my oldest son, Drew, who knows "the deep, dark secret," is speaking of Santa Claus in tones of faith again. This is the season when magic overcomes reason and credit cards overwhelm good sense. It's a great time of year!

As I write these words, I am staring at my children's Christmas lists. They write them each year with multiple revisions, deletions, and frantic last-minute additions. This is serious stuff.

I've saved their lists over the years. There is something vulnerable and precious about their childish wishes. They are giving away the secrets of their heart.

I reflect back on my own childhood. My father was a big, tender-hearted guy who could be tough and gruff but would give you the shirt off of his back. He spoiled my sister and me rotten at Christmas. Dad and Mom loved to give gifts, and we received with extravagance.

Once my nine-year-old son, Luke, asked me, "Dad, what was your favoritist present you ever got given?"

I didn't hesitate: "It was my Lionel train, the big yellow and black Rio Grande engine I saved for you and Drew. No question about it. That was the best Christmas present of all time."

"How old were you when you got it?"

"I was eight. It was the Christmas of 1958. We were living in the Philippines. I can still see the orange and blue cardboard boxes the train came in. I can smell the oil and electricity when

42 the engine warmed up and charged around the track. My first train will always be my favorite present."

"Well," Luke continued, "did you ever ask Santa Claus for something you didn't get?"

Pausing, I looked wise and pursed my lips, "Yep, I asked for a pony one time when I was four and didn't get it."

"Why not?"

"Well, probably because we lived in the city and had a small back yard. No room for a horse."

"Is that the only thing you never got that you asked for?"

"Nope," I sagely replied. "Once when I was ten I asked for a shotgun, but Santa knew I wasn't old enough yet. I guess he knew I'd hurt myself or shoot somebody. I got a BB gun instead."

"Well, Dad, do you think I'll get everything on my list this year?" Luke broke in, getting down to the real issue.

"I don't know. But I do know Santa Claus will be good to you. He always is."

Luke walked out of my study reassured while I grew a little sad. It won't be long until the beard falls off of Santa in this little boy's life and the truth sinks in.

Somehow the quest for Santa Claus never leaves us. And when time and maturity inevitably explode the myth, we are prone to hang the long, white beard and red stocking hat on God. For many sophisticated adults, God becomes the Santa Claus in the sky. And prayer to God is an endless litany of what we want and what we need. We keep a list of what we get and what we don't. And when our prayers are not answered, we raise the question, "Why?"

I believe that Jesus Christ came to dispel the Santa myth; to differentiate between the fable of Santa Claus and the reality of God. And he did so by simply calling God "Father."

Perhaps one of the most important Bible passages in relationship to the identity of God and the nature of prayer is Matthew 7:9-11. Jesus says to his disciples: "Is there anyone among you who, if your child asks for bread, will give a stone?

Or if the child asks for a fish, will give a snake? If you then, who 43 are evil, know how to give good gifts to your children, how much more will your Father in heaven give good things to those who ask him!"

What Jesus' words say to me is that you and I request from God a lot of things that could really hurt us. Like children, we are sincere in what we ask and genuinely believe that it is the best thing for us. We are hungry for something and we pursue our desires. But often we are like a toddler asking for a shotgun.

I fondly remember falling head over heels in love during college. I was sure that this beautiful young woman was the one with whom God intended for me to spend the rest of my life. Miraculously, she was of the same opinion. I began to pray earnestly that we might get married some day. It was obvious to me that my desire was in the will of God. I was hungry and asking for bread. Would God give me a stone or a snake? Certainly not.

Well, despite my prayers and earnest intentions, we did not get married. A year later we broke up in a tangle of confusing, painful, and perplexing emotions. Now looking back from the vantage point of twenty years of a happy marriage, I know that I would have not been the best mate for that lovely woman. A caring God led us in different directions, used our broken relationship to make us wiser, and gave to us what we really wanted, fulfilling marriages.

Quite simply, God will give to us the deepest desires of our heart. But God will not give to us what will hurt us. And he will not always grant what makes perfectly logical sense to us.

Many times I have prayed for sick children to live and they have died. I have prayed for wars to end and they have continued to wage their carnage. I have prayed for Christians to stop fighting each other, for churches to heal, and marriages to mend. Yet conflict has continued. Where is God in my reasonable prayers for mercy and peace?

I don't have an answer. My mind is not great enough to understand truth on God's level. And my perspective is so very

44   limited in terms of the infinite and what lies beyond this short life. But two things I do know. First, God never causes pain and sorrow. And, second, God is constantly working for the very best for all of us. One day we will reach a vantage point where even tragedy, conflict, and pain will make sense. But that is one day. Not now.

For now we must simply be our human selves. As children, we can be honest and naively open with our requests unto God. And, like my father, God will chuckle with delight when we ask for a pony or a shotgun. There is something about our earnest and innocent sharing that is endearing to our Father.

But God will give only that which is good. This Jesus knew for certain. And for this reason he could grit his teeth on the worst day of his life and cry, "My father, if it is possible, let this cup pass from Me; yet not as I will, but as Thou wilt."

As with Jesus, God takes our crucifixions and creates resurrections. And he takes prayers that are honest but foolish and ultimately gives to us the deepest desires of our heart. We must be patient because we will fully glimpse God's goodness only from the far side of eternity. And when in our ignorance we ask for rocks and snakes, we can be assured that he will give us bread and fish.

And this is the boldness we have in him, that if we ask anything according to his will, he hears us. And if we know that he hears us in whatever we ask, we know that we have obtained the requests made of him.
1 JOHN 5:14-15

You ask and do not receive, because you ask wrongly, in order to spend what you get on your pleasures.
JAMES 4:3

A thorn was given me in the flesh, a messenger of Satan to torment me, to keep me from being to elated. Three times I appealed to the Lord about this, that it would leave me, but he said to me, "My grace is sufficient for you, for power is made perfected in weakness." So, I will boast all the more gladly of my weaknesses, so that the power of Christ may dwell in me.
    2 CORINTHIANS 12:7-9

Likewise the Spirit helps us in our weakness; for we do not know how to pray as we ought, but that very Spirit intercedes with sighs too deep for words. And God, who searches the heart, knows what is the mind of the Spirit, because the Spirit intercedes for the saints according to the will of God. We know that all things work together for good for those who love God, who are called according to his purpose.
    ROMANS 8:26-28

One obvious reason for our unanswered petitions is, of course, the ignorance of our asking. Piety is no guarantee of wisdom. . . . Indeed, instead of calling prayers unanswered, it is far truer to recognize that "No" is as real an answer as "Yes," and often far more kind. When one considers the partialness of our knowledge, the narrowness of our outlook, our little skill in tracing the far-off consequences of our desire, he sees how often God must speak to us, as Jesus did to the ambitious woman, "Ye know not what ye ask" (Matthew 20:22).[1]
    HARRY EMERSON FOSDICK

What discord should we bring into the universe if our prayers were all answered. Then we should govern the world and not God. And do you think we should govern it better? It gives me only pain when I hear the long, wearisome petitions of men asking for they know not what. . . .

Thanksgiving with a full heart—and the rest silence and submission to the divine will![2]
    HENRY WADSWORTH LONGFELLOW

Does [Matthew 7:7-8] mean that if you pray hard enough you can get anything you want? Is Jesus saying that God is a celestial Santa Claus who always brings good little boys and girls what they ask for? Surely not. It simply is not true that you can work up to such a stage of influence upon God that you wrangle anything in the world out of him. He isn't a Heavenly Vending Machine that is set in motion by a ten-cent prayer.[3]
    CLARENCE JORDAN

Dear God, I am thankful that when we talk I do not need to measure my words; to choose them carefully and later worry about what I have said. I know that because you are my Father, I can ramble and sound half-baked.

There will be some days, Lord, when I am talking out of my head: enraged by a slight, blinded by pain, biased by ignorance, inflamed and enticed by the Evil One. O God, take me in stride. Listen and grant what is good. And forget what is bad or foolish. I am a child. And my greatest wisdom is prattle in your sight.

Thank you, Lord, that with you I can be myself. That you enjoy my company and conversation. And thanks, above all, that you will provide for my every need. Amen.

HORNS AND BUCKETS

SEVERAL YEARS AGO I FOUND MYSELF IN a jeep bumping across the rugged mountainous interior of Jamaica. Dr. John Trotter, an American physician, was driving, and we were participating together in a medical mission project. Rounding a narrow corner, John suddenly slammed on the brakes. Jolted, we came face to face with a rather wide-eyed but complacent cow munching grass in the middle of the rutted road.

Coasting to a stop five feet from her bony flank, John blew the horn. With a jerk the cow lifted her head and bellowed but refused to move. Exasperated at her stubbornness, we began to yell at her. The old bovine seemed to want to beat a hasty retreat but couldn't get herself in gear. Finally, John jumped out of the jeep, intending to be more persuasive.

Rounding the front fender, John came to an abrupt halt. He stared at the ground and then began to laugh. Returning to the driver's seat and ramming the gear shift into reverse, he chuckled, "We could have blown the horn all day and that cow wouldn't have moved! We're parked on her chain!"

As soon as the jeep rolled backward, the old cow reverted to her youth and bolted across the road, ripping her stake from the ground and dragging the chain behind her. We had set her free.

Sometimes when I pray, I find myself thinking of this ridiculous scene. Often I want things to happen in my life: some situation to change, a problem to be solved, an obstacle to be removed from my path. As my frustration grows, I blow my

40

I fondly ask. But Patience, to prevent
That murmur, soon replies: "God doth not need
Either man's work or his own gifts; who best
Bear his mild yoke, they serve him best. His state
Is kingly; thousands at his bidding speed,
And post o'er land and ocean without rest;
They also serve who only stand and wait." [3]
   JOHN MILTON

Dear Lord, so much of life is spent in waiting. Waiting and knocking on closed doors. "What a waste of precious time!" I shout at the heavens. There are better things to do.

Calm me down, Lord. Help me to see that you know the right moment. The right place. I am not squandering time because you are preparing me, shaping me, training me for what lies ahead.

Accept my bruised knuckles as a symbol that I love you. May I trust that you have heard the beating of my heart long before the knocking of my hand. Amen.

the chain. I can pray about writing this book all that I want but until I sit down and wrestle with words, God cannot help me.

Yet, what a partnership there is with the Spirit of God when we finally "get with it!" Suddenly the Helper is present and we are enabled to do the task before us. What is truly wonderful about God is that he really cares—not just about the big things, but about the little things, too.

The Greeks of Jesus' day had a favorite adjective they used to describe the gods of Olympus. It is a word from which we derive our English word *apathetic*. They truly felt the gods could best be characterized by cold unconcern and insensitivity to the needs of humankind.

In contrast, Jesus taught that God is intimately concerned about the life and situation of each individual: "Are not two sparrows sold for a penny? And not one of them will fall to the ground without your Father's will. But even the hairs of your head are all numbered. Fear not, therefore; you are of more value than many sparrows" (Matthew 10:29-31, Phillips).

Jesus teaches us that God is not apathetic and content to abandon us to our own work and problem solving. To the contrary, God is concerned and involved in all that we do. But God can do little for us if we are parked on the chain of progress.

For me, today is the day to quit honking and pass the buckets. How about you?

Commit your work to the Lord, and your plans will be established.
PROVERBS 16:3

But Jesus answered them, "My Father is still working, and I also am working."
JOHN 5:17

For even when we were with you, we gave you this command: Anyone unwilling to work should not eat. For we hear that some of you are living in idleness, mere busybodies, not doing any work. Now such persons we command and exhort in the Lord Jesus Christ to do their work quietly and to earn their own living.

2 THESSALONIANS 3:10-12

There are prayers . . . which attempt to accomplish by supplication what can be accomplished only by work.[1]

HARRY EMERSON FOSDICK

The monastic orders, such as the Rule of St. Benedict, wisely insisted on a discipline of manual and mental toil. Man is set for his growth in an unfinished earth—its fields at first weed-cluttered, its gold held in mountain-ore, its homes mere scattered stones, and its songs and pictures only inchoate in dream and hope. This seems to be by deliberate intent. We learn by labor, nor can we rightly expect our prayers to spare us that discipline.[2]

GEORGE ARTHUR BUTTRICK

As a youth I had been woefully at fault, particularly in early adolescence. I had prayed to you for chastity and said, "Give me chastity and continence, but not yet!" For I was afraid that you would answer my prayer at once and cure me too soon of the disease of lust, which I wanted satisfied, not quelled.[3]

ST. AUGUSTINE

Is it not very often the fear of having to let go of something that holds us back from honest prayer and meditation? God leads us only when we are really ready to let go.[4]

PAUL TOURNIER

Dear God, it is far too easy to pray when pressures and deadlines catch up with me. I want to escape, to scream for help, to barter for a quick solution. Prayer can be an easy way out.

Yet, Lord, I am glad that the desire to pray comes naturally. Perhaps through prayer I can ask that you make me more industrious, more disciplined, better organized. I do not desire that I become obsessed and driven . . . a grim, dour, workaholic. But I ask that I be enabled to take one step at a time, working each day to the best of my ability.

I trust that my work and your guidance will blend together to accomplish the purposes that we both desire. May we co-create together in a world where work becomes pleasure. Amen.

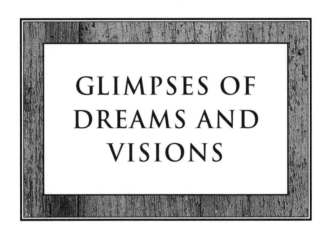

GLIMPSES OF DREAMS AND VISIONS

THE BIRTH
OF DREAMS

I HAD A WONDERFUL CHILDHOOD growing up in the Philippine Islands. We had no television to watch or shopping malls filled with toy stores and glitzy distractions. There were no Little League baseball or football games. But there was the vast and lush beauty of nature to explore and a world filled with surprises.

We lived on the island of Luzon on the ridge of a range of mountains that towered a mile high. Streams cascaded down steep slopes covered in thick pine forests and raced through the narrow canyon floors. Much of the land was sparsely inhabited, and you could wander for hours without seeing another person.

It was a safe place to grow up. My mother could kiss me goodbye on a summer morning and set me free to ramble and explore, not expecting to see me again until the sun had set. There was a wild and rich freedom to my childhood.

As a ten year old, I had developed a wanderlust and a vivid imagination. During the monsoon season, I loved to huddle by our fireplace and read Hardy Boys mysteries and devour *National Geographic* magazines as the rain hammered down on our tin roof. I was keenly aware of a vast world to explore, and I itched to make my own discoveries.

My buddies and I were mesmerized by the fact that deep within the Luzon Mountains were rich deposits of gold. Many mines dotted the rugged landscape, and tons of ore were

56 extracted each year. There was a fortune out there to be made and we dreamed of discovering gold.

My friend Kenny and I read all that we could about panning for gold. Raiding my mother's pots and pans drawer, we would pack our army surplus knapsacks with sandwiches and cookies, fill our canteens with water, strap a hunting knife, machete, and hatchet on our belts, hang binoculars and a compass on our necks, and head off for the deep tropical forest in the valley below.

One day Kenny and I were miles from home and winding our way through a stretch of dense woods we had never explored. Earlier we had heard the roar of a stream in the distance and had been trying to locate it for the last hour. Leaving the faint path we had been following, we were now hacking our way through dense brush and fighting the fear of getting lost. I had a ten year old's awareness that I was severely pushing my boundaries of safety.

Fighting our way through one last strand of undergrowth, we burst into a clearing and the stream lay before us. My mouth fell open in amazement and wonder. This was not just any stream. This was a picture of absolute beauty and wonder.

Thirty feet above us the stream gushed out of the side of a sheer rock precipice. Surging forth from its concealed subterranean course, the water was cascading down the mountainside and splashing into a deep pool surrounded by lush, green ferns. Out of the pool the stream continued to flow, making its way through the forest and on to its destiny in the South China Sea. It was a scene of primal beauty that stirs in me feelings of awe and joy thirty-four years later.

"Kenny, this has got to be it," I blurted excitedly. "The river's coming right out of the mountain. It's gotta have gold in it."

Throwing down our packs, we grabbed our pans and waded out into the cold, bracing water. Much to my astonishment we didn't need the pans. All around us on the floor of the clear pool were rocks studded with flecks of gold. Picking them up and watching the yellow veins glitter in the warm sun's light brought

screams of excitement from two wild-eyed boys. We had done it!
We had struck it rich! We had discovered gold!

Gazing at our watches, we knew that we had to hurry to find our way back home before dark. Gathering as many gold-laced rocks as we could, we stuffed them in our knapsacks, staggering under their weight, and made our way back up the mountain side. At each turn we placed a mark on a tree with our machete, etching the route in our memory so that we would not lose this treasure lode. Sloshing around in our wet tennis shoes, we raced homeward

Just as the last rays of sunlight were swallowed by night, we trooped into our yard, yelling at the top of our lungs. The silhouette of my father could be seen standing on the front porch waiting for us!

"Son, where have you been?" his worried voice barked. "You and Kenny shouldn't be gone so long without checking in."

Not stopping to apologize, Kenny and I screamed, "We found gold! We're rich! Really rich!"

Rushing into the house, we gathered around the kitchen sink and unloaded our treasure of gold-studded rocks onto the counter. Washing the largest, I proudly held it up to show my father. Taking it in his large hands, he walked over to the bright lamp by his easy chair, sat down, and slowly examined the rock.

Kenny and I stood beside him in the shadows, holding our breaths and waiting for his own excitement to burst forth. He was silent. Painfully silent. Then slowly he began to smile.

"I can see why you guys are so excited. This stuff really looks like gold. But what I think you've found is pyrite, or "fool's gold." Fools gold has snookered a lot of people. It's a mineral deposit layered in rock, but it's not real gold. Just looks like it. When I was a boy growing up in Colorado, there were a lot of prospectors that were taken by this stuff."

When Dad looked up, he saw two boys whose faces said it all. We were crushed. I stood in the shadows fighting back tears. I felt childish and embarrassed—and, above all, disappointed.

"Well, it's not the end of the world," Dad said, grabbing us both and hauling us squirming into his lap. "One thing's for sure, fool's gold or not, there's real gold out there somewhere. You ought to go right back tomorrow and look even harder. Everybody has to pan a lot of fool's gold before they find the real thing. And you can do it."

Rumpling our sweaty hair, he rolled us out of the chair into a heap on the floor. Laughing, he looked at the glinting rock and royally decreed, "Fool's gold is better than no gold at all!" Kenny and I finally broke into smiles.

That scene is a touchstone, an epiphany, an encounter with truth that I have relived over and over. For when it comes right down to it, what we were really talking about that night was not so much gold as it was dreams and visions, the real treasure chest of life.

More precious than gold is the dream behind finding the gold or whatever glimmering vision or quest calls you forth into life. Now, in the midst of adulthood, I wish I could again dredge up that untarnished exuberance that compels a youth to strap on a machete, follow a compass, and confidently forge into the unknown of rich discovery.

My dad must have known the power and risk of the psychic dynamite he was dealing with that night. To quash the dreams of children—or adults—is to take their life force away. Dreams are the energy and vitality of existence.

My father did not ridicule my dreams, he nourished them: "Go right back tomorrow, Son, and look even harder. You can find it!" Holding fool's gold in his hands, he placed true gold in my heart, his blessing of my aspirations, dreams and visions.

Langston Hughes once wrote: "Hold fast to dreams, for if dreams die, life is a broken winged bird that cannot fly."

Hughes reflects the wisdom of the ages. The task of adulthood is to keep our dreams alive. Many dreams must be inevitably altered to fit reality. Forks in the roads will soon be reached where

we must painfully choose between equally desirable options. Disillusionment is a bitter gall we all must drink. But behind it all
there must be a dream. And we must not let go of it.

Adapt our dream, yes. But not bury it. Not let it die. Not
become a broken winged bird that cannot fly.

The simple truth is that most of us do find a lot of fool's gold
before we discover the real thing. But the journey of exploration
is exciting. And fool's gold will teach us to recognize the real
thing when its glint is finally seen.

Kenny and I never discovered gold, though we sought it with
all of our heart. But we found something infinitely more valu-
able. We discovered the power of dreams and visions, fantasy
and imagination, ideals and virtues, that point far beyond the
pathway of this life and into the vast unknown of eternity.

Where there is no vision, the people perish.
PROVERBS 29:18

Then afterward
I will pour out my spirit on all flesh;
your sons and your daughters shall prophecy,
your old men shall dream dreams,
and your young men shall see visions.
Even on the male and female servants
in those days, I will pour out my spirit.
JOEL 2:28-29

Grown-up people reconcile themselves too willingly to a
supposed duty of preparing young ones for the time when
they will regard as illusion what now is an inspiration to
heart and mind. Deeper experience of life, however,
advises their inexperience differently. It exhorts them to
hold fast, their whole life through, to the thoughts which

inspire them. It is through the idealism of youth that man catches sight of truth, and in that idealism he possesses a wealth which he must never exchange for anything else....

The power of ideals is incalculable. We see no power in a drop of water. But let it get into a crack in the rock and be turned to ice, and it splits the rock; turned into steam, it drives the pistons of the most powerful engines. Something has happened to it which makes active and effective the power that is latent in it.[1]

ALBERT SCHWEITZER

It must be borne in mind that the tragedy of life doesn't lie in not reaching your goal. The tragedy lies in having no goal to reach. It isn't a calamity to die with dreams unfulfilled, but it is a calamity not to dream.[2]

BENJAMIN E. MAYS

During the first period of a man's life the greatest danger is: not to take the risk.[3]

SØREN KIERKEGAARD

I do not know why it is that we remember so much about some of the small decisions of our lives and so little about most of the great ones, but for me at least that has always tended to be the case. Maybe it is because the great decisions are not made at some particular moment in time but deep within us have been so long in the making that we find ourselves acting on them before we are altogether conscious of having decided to.[4]

FREDERICK BUECHNER

Lord, I want my life to count for something; I want to know that my years will be filled with purpose and meaning. I don't want to simply exist, to mark time. I yearn to live for reasons bigger than dollars and cents, fleeting fame, or fragile security. I long to take the risk, attempt the quest, whatever it might be.

Father, you are both Creator and Sustainer. Years ago you created a Dream in me. Now sustain me. Enable me to discern the tasks before me, to know the difference between challenge and folly, to believe that my life can make a difference.

May your Spirit fill me so that, young or old, I may dream dreams and see visions. Amen.

THE CUP

THE WALKER FAMILY HAD BEEN TRAVEL-
ing for decades. No one knows who that first brave soul was who
left England for the American colonies. But once his feet touched
the sand of the Carolina shore, he and his descendants followed
the sun westward.

They trekked across the Carolinas, chased by poverty and
lured by the prospect of free and better land. Reaching Tennessee,
they floated down the Tennessee River, occasionally stopping to
rest and recoup in a rustic settlement until the wanderlust got
hold of them again. By the 1820s, they had followed the course of
the Tennessee River north into Kentucky until this wild river
flowed into the Ohio River and on into the Illinois territory.

Stopping in Illinois for a only a few years, the family again
built flat boats and floated down the Mississippi until they came
to the mouth of the White River in Arkansas. For reasons now
unknown, they decided that this remote spot on God's green
earth would become their home. At last the generations had
found a stopping place, a place to own land and build houses and
raise children, a place to survive the tragedy of the American
Civil War, a place to watch more than one generation grow old.

My grandfather was the third generation of this Walker family to live in Arkansas. Tall, lean, and raw boned, Eddie Benjamin
Walker worked in his father's fields as a small boy, going to
school only between planting and harvesting when his father
could spare him. Though life was largely arduous labor, there

were also moments of fun. Fishing was every man's escape, and 63
landing the giant alligator garfish was exotic adventure. Saturday
night dances to the tune of a fiddle, energized by the elixir of
moonshine whiskey and youthful hormones, set the stage for
much excitement, romance, and many a brawl. It was wild country and tough people.

Strangely, my grandfather met my grandmother, Callie
Weatherly, not at a raucous dance but in a church, a place Walk-
ers avoided. Coerced into escorting a girlfriend to choir practice,
Eddie sat stiffly and ill at ease on the back bench waiting for the
ordeal to be over. That's when he first spotted Callie in the choir
and fell head over heels in love.

They weren't much older than kids when they got married
and quickly began to have children. They lived with Eddie's parents for a year, yearning for privacy. Finally enough lumber was
cut and cured to build their own house, and they moved two hundred yards away, across a dirt road in the midst of an oak grove.
It was a short distance but a giant leap toward independence.

Callie kept going to the Friendship Church, walking a mile
down a rutted road to the white planked building framed by a
cemetery atop a grassy knoll. Two Sundays each month the
Methodist circuit rider preached and exhorted, while the other
two Sundays a Baptist preacher blistered the air with themes of
salvation and judgment.

Eddie still didn't like church. Marriage hadn't changed that.
Sunday was his only day to sleep, rest, and fish. But as a new husband he had not yet learned to say no to his headstrong wife. He
trudged beside her "to preaching" chafing like a young stallion
under bridle and bit. Before he knew it, he was corralled. The old
Baptist preacher held him over the fires of hell, pummeled him
under conviction, dunked him in a muddy river, and left him to
stagger from the experience a baptized Christian. Not knowing
what all the fuss was about, Eddie needed a few years to grow
into the meaning of his Christian birthing. But he matured and
mellowed with age, his faith becoming the stackpole of his life.

Ten years and four kids later, Eddie was twenty-eight and tired of living in the midst of a clan composed of a dominant father, three brothers, and a mob of assorted uncles, aunts, and cousins. The family was comfortable but smothering. The inherited wanderlust of bygone patriarchs began to course through his veins, and he thought about following the sun, moving west.

That's when the house burned down. A spring tornado had narrowly missed Eddie's house, shaking it every way but loose and damaging the chimney. Somehow a spark lodged in the chimney wall where mortar had crumbled. It smoldered between brick and wood overnight and burst into flame while Eddie was plowing and Callie was washing her long dark hair. The house became an inferno in minutes. All was lost. Everything, that is, except the most important thing, life itself. Possessions were destroyed but the family survived.

Callie's health broke, however. Maybe it was the stress of loss and maybe not. But the old country doctor said it was the climate. The river bottom land, he opined, was too humid, causing rheumatism, headaches, and just about anything else that ailed you. He told Eddie that if his young wife was going to live to see her children married, he needed to move to a drier climate.

Eddie smiled behind his grimace. He'd been thinking about moving anyway. He was a young man with a head full of dreams, and dreams wouldn't happen if he stood still. He was too fenced in. Like his forefathers, he needed to break away, set his own course, find a place where land was cheap, and start all over.

The place he found was the Great Plains of northeastern Colorado. Land there was a giveaway. Nobody in their right mind wanted it. It was desolate and arid country, flat as a shaved board. You had to be tough and a little crazy to live there. But it was a chance. A chance to own dark, rich, virgin soil—and a lot of it. A chance to start all over. Eddie Walker dreamed of ranching and farming under big blue vibrant sky.

Eddie and his older brother, John, moved their families by train to Flagler, Colorado. They precut wood for their houses

from the lush forests of Arkansas and shipped the hardwood
planks to Colorado in a boxcar along with braying mules, plows, and barrels of flour and sorghum. They built John's house before winter roared in and huddled together through blizzards. It was brutal weather unlike any they had known. But they survived. Callie began to secretly think that the sinus headaches of Arkansas weren't half as bad as the bleak loneliness of the prairie.

When spring finally came, Eddie built his house, harnessed the mules, and plowed the first furrow the soil had ever known. Though he smiled and exulted in the pristine barrenness, he noted that his brother and sister-in-law were increasingly unhappy. Before long, John sold out and moved on to Oregon, a land that was green and wet like Arkansas. Eddie and Callie were left to go it alone.

Somewhere in those first few years of hard-scrabble survival, a final child was born, a boy named Al, who was to become my father. He was a son of Colorado, a child of the plains, a boy who saw in the buffalo land a deep beauty and did not compare life to Arkansas.

Years moved on and Eddie and Callie were successful. By the 1930s, they farmed large tracts of land and had developed a herd of five hundred head of fine Hereford cattle. Though the great depression was shaking the economic foundations of the country, Eddie thought he could make it. What he wasn't counting on was dying.

It happened one morning when my father, now fourteen, and his Dad rode into town on a wagon for supplies. Walking down the street, Eddie suddenly fainted. A medicine he was taking for "stomach trouble" had eaten through his stomach wall. Peritonitis set in, and his forty-eight years of life came to a sudden and tragic end.

Economics has no respect for persons, and the Great Depression continued to bear down on the family. Soon Callie and her sons had to decide whether to sell their cattle for little profit or shoot them to keep them from starving. Though the

66   homestead was paid for, the wolf was growling viciously at the door. It was bleak and perilous times.

Amidst the struggle, my father, Al, could feel a teenage dream stirring within him. He loved the plains and ranching. He was tough and hardy and a cowboy at heart. But he also had discovered that he loved education, reading about a wider world, and exploring the philosophical questions of life. He became enamored by his young pastor, Reverend Peterson, who encouraged him to study hard, dig deep, and pursue his dreams. When he graduated from high school, my father put all that he owned in a locker trunk and took off for California to go to college.

Except for short visits, Dad never went back. An older brother ran the ranch for several years, but finally it was sold. Another generation was cast off to float down new rivers, dream new dreams, and see where life would lead them.

In my eyes, my father was a great man. He had a vision and pursued it without reservation. Earning a Ph.D. in theology, he became a pastor and then a missionary in the Philippines. He explored the spiritual mysteries of life and crossed broader rivers than he ever dreamed possible as a small boy in Colorado. Tragically, he contracted a tropical blood disease that resulted in a fatal heart attack when he was forty-six. But he crowded in a lot of living and fulfilled a lot of dreams in a short period of time. He lived life to the fullest. I loved him dearly, and I still do.

As I write these words, tears well up in my eyes. Through their prism I look up and spot our antique breakfront china cabinet. It is where special family treasures are kept: my mother's childhood tea set, a collection of leather-bound books, souvenirs of family trips. But most valued of all is a simple white and flowered china cup. Though the cup has a special history, its symbolic import is for the future.

When the ranch was sold in Colorado before I was born, there wasn't much for brothers and sisters to inherit. On a kitchen shelf sat my grandfather's favorite cup from which he drank his coffee early each morning, waiting for the sun to rise. My father took the cup and carefully packed it in his suitcase. It would be his one memento from childhood, his symbol of the past. The cup was what I in turn inherited as a teenager when my father died.

What does this cup mean to me? Sometimes I think about the Colorado ranch and wonder what it would have been like if things had been different. The land is worth a fortune now, prime wheat fields in the fertile heart of America. What if Eddie had lived a good, long life and there had been no Depression? We might be rich as kings right now, heirs to a great farming and ranching dynasty. Maybe so. Maybe not.

Fantasy aside, all that is tangibly left to show for generations upon generations of toil and struggle is one, solitary china cup. What is the meaning of this symbolism? Where is the power of its ironic message?

Holding the cup in my hands, the one thing that is apparent is that the cup is empty. I have learned that each generation must fill their own cup. It cannot be done for you.

And yet, there is a cup—something that enables you to hold the fluid dream of life between your hands and drink deeply of its richness. My cup of inheritance has been made from the substance of religious faith and the example of parents who believed that their life could make a difference in this world. The cup is not something material, not something I can inherit through a will or trust. Rather, the cup is something that can only be lived out and exemplified from one generation to another. The cup is made from the clay of character and fired in the kiln of experience. The cup is what allows the next generation to hold the waters of life in their hands and not let its vitality and opportunity dribble through their outstretched fingers. And yet, the cup is empty. And it always must be. The cup of life must be filled anew with the dreams and aspirations of each new generation. The previous generation cannot fill it for them.

Living amidst the most affluent generation America has ever known—the result of standing on the shoulders of countless generations before us—we are tempted to give our children

68   everything. Yet, what a tragedy it is to attempt to give to them a full cup, even if we could. It robs them of the hunger for life, a healthy sense of ambition and creativity, the very substance that leads to contribution and character. We cannot, we should not, give them everything. They must float down their own rivers, carve out their own land, and face the uncertainty and challenges of their unique future as each generation before them has done. Above all, they must dream their dreams and seek their visions—not our dreams and not our visions. They must fill the cup themselves if they are to be satisfied with its substance.

But we can give them a cup. Just a cup and no more. And that cup must be the fragile shell from which we drink of character, example, faith, hope, and love. They will need nothing more. They must receive nothing less.

The Lord is my chosen portion and my cup . . .
    PSALM 16:5

Train children in the right way,
and when old, they will not stray.
    PROVERBS 22:6

Then Jesus told his disciples, "If any want to become my followers, let them deny themselves and take up their cross and follow me. For those who want to save their life will lose it, and those who lose their life for my sake will find it. For what will it profit them if they gain the whole world but forfeit their life? Or what will they give in return for their life?
    MATTHEW 16:24-26

Peter began to say to him, "Look, we have left everything and followed you." Jesus said, "Truly I tell you, there is no

one who has left house or brothers or sisters or mother or father or children or fields, for my sake and for the sake of the good news, who will not receive a hundredfold now in this age—houses, brothers and sisters, mothers and children and fields with persecutions—and in the age to come, eternal life. But many who are first will be last, and the last will be first."
MARK 10:28-30

Children have never been very good at listening to their elders, but they have never failed to imitate them.[1]
JAMES BALDWIN

When our main concern is to shield people from pain, we will produce little more than hothouse plants who cannot make it in the real world. Much of the truth that becomes existentially our own grows out of our wounds.[2]
JOHN CLAYPOOL

I asked for strength that I might achieve;
I was made weak that I might learn humbly to obey.
I asked for health that I might do greater things;
I was given infirmity that I might do better things.
I asked for riches that I might be happy;
I was given poverty that I might be wise.
I asked for power that I might have the praise of men;
I was given weakness that I might feel the need of God.
I asked for all things that I might enjoy life;
I was given life that I might enjoy all things.
I got nothing that I had asked for,
but everything that I had hoped for.
Almost despite myself my unspoken prayers were answered;
I am, among all men, most richly blessed.[3]
AN UNKNOWN CONFEDERATE SOLDIER
UNITED STATES CIVIL WAR, 1861-1865

Dear God, as a sweet breath from childhood, I remember the words of the Psalmist:

> Lord, Thou hast been our dwelling place
>   in all generations.
> Before the mountains were born,
> Or Thou didst give birth to the earth and the world,
> Even from everlasting to everlasting Thou art God.
> (Psalm 90:1-2, KJV)

I hear my Father intone these words as a call to worship on countless Sundays in now forgotten places. The memories fade but the words have been hid in my heart. They are a compass for a traveler, a glimpse of light in the night. They are the cup of my inheritance.

Whatever my life's dream, O Lord, may it be grounded in you. May the desires of my heart and the passions of my soul reflect the Spirit of Christ.

Grant that I may be able to give to those who come after me the same cup of inheritance that was bequeathed to me. Regardless of their future circumstance, may you fill their cup with faith, hope, joy and love. May each generation learn above all else that "from everlasting to everlasting Thou art God." Amen.

DREAMS AND CONTENTMENT

IT WAS A COLD AND RAINY DAY, LOUSY weather for a funeral. Having finished the funeral service in the sanctuary, I was hustling to my car, fumbling with my umbrella, concentrating on what I would say at graveside. Through the whirl of my thoughts I heard Elizabeth's voice: "Why don't you ride with us, Scott? We're going to a country cemetery and you might get lost. And we don't need you getting lost!" Smiling, I agreed and slipped into the backseat of her car.

Elizabeth Alexander was in her sixties, a pretty woman who exudes quality and poise. Dick, her husband, was on the faculty at the University of Georgia. Several days before, after spending the day hoeing his garden, Elizabeth's elderly father had died quietly while resting in a bench swing under the shade of an oak tree. Today we were laying him to rest in the Georgia soil he had plowed and farmed for years.

As Dick drove out of the city limits of Athens and into the countryside, I looked at Elizabeth and said, "Tell me a little more about your dad. He sounds like a delightful person."

"Daddy was great," Elizabeth replied. "He was a loving man and a real character." Then she got a far-away look in her eye and started laughing.

"I remember the time Daddy bought the shrimp boat," she chuckled. "Craziest thing he ever did. When we were children, he'd take us to the beach for vacation. While we'd swim and sit in the sun, he'd stroll the shore and watch the shrimp boats on the horizon. He'd go down to the docks in the afternoon when the shrimpers came in and watch them unload their catch. Somehow he got it into his head that owning and operating a shrimp boat would be the best thing in the world.

"Well, the idea wouldn't let go of him. He didn't talk much about it. But there were those hot, humid summer days when he'd be on his tractor eating dust and he'd think of those shrimp boats. It nearly drove him crazy.

"I guess we all knew that he was getting tired of farming, but we never expected him to sell the farm. He did. When he came home and told us we were all moving to the coast, we thought he was crazy. But we got excited—real excited!

"Well, we did move, and Dad finally bought his shrimp boat. Didn't know a thing about shrimping but it was the proudest day of his life. He hired a crew and started a new career.

"Didn't last long, though," Elizabeth chuckled. "Daddy found out he got seasick, sick as a dog. He thought he'd get over it or get used to it, but he never did. Every day he'd come back green around the gills. Soon all of the fun drained out of his life. Before long he sold the boat, moved back home, and bought another farm. After that, he always liked farming a lot better. Kinda found peace in his soul. I never heard him complain again."

When I heard this story, the ring of truth pealed forth. I recognized that the old farmer that I was to bury was very much alive within me. Though I've never plowed a furrow or longed to own a shrimp boat, I know what it means to be torn between the drivenness of dreams and the spiritual need for contentment.

It is true, dreams are a primal source of life. Without desires and ambition, our existence becomes flat and listless. Life ebbs away. We all need the vital spirit of a Don Quixote jousting within us. The importance of "dreaming the impossible dream" is vital to the human soul. Our reach must exceed our grasp.

But there is another side to this complex equation. Life is perfectly miserable if we can never be content with who we are and what we possess due to our own insatiable drivenness toward what we are not and what we do not possess. The farmer could not enjoy the green beauty of lush and fertile farm land because he craved the blue expanse of the ocean and the wild pounding sea.

Most of us get caught in this dilemma. For instance, as young adults many of us dreamed of owning a house. We grew tired of the nomadic life of apartment dwelling. We wanted stability and roots. With our hearts in our throats, we signed the mortgage papers and thrust our necks into a tight financial noose. But fear aside, we were happy. Happy with the little two-bedroom bungalow and the postage stamp yard, happy with the roof that leaked and the fuses that blew every time we plugged in the hairdryer. It was not the perfect house but it was our house and we were happy.

Happy, that is, until we got a raise, grew comfortable with house payments, became more bold, and started driving around in other neighborhoods. Then the one house that we loved wasn't good enough anymore—not big enough, nice enough, practical enough, expensive enough. It was time to sell the farm and move to the ocean.

Again, many of us have thought for years that professional success would make us happy. Slowly we climbed the ladder and planted our feet on the highest rung. Though in that thin air there was satisfaction and excitement, there was also a sick feeling in the pit of our stomachs. Rather than being filled with contentment, we felt a gnawing emptiness in our souls. With Coleridge's ancient mariner we looked at the vast ocean we had successfully sailed and shouted against the heavens, "Water, water, everywhere, but not a drop to drink!"

An ancient oriental parable tells of a man riding in the night, searching for his lost ox, unaware that he is riding the ox he is searching for. How true this has often been of my life. All I could ever want I have today. I am sitting on it! Riding the fat back of fullness right now! But somehow I am persuaded that happiness and fulfillment is always out there somewhere. Never here. Always there. Only a dream away.

...an beat myself over the head, I have come to realize ...erson must buy a shrimp boat sometime (perhaps, ...es!) in his or her life. And we all must become seasick until we long for the stability of shore once more. The... no substitute for experience. Only through mistakes and disillusionment can we begin to learn the lessons of contentment. Only then can we begin to ponder the paradox of our absolute need for dreams and the spiritual demand for contentment and acceptance.

A long time ago I buried an old farmer in the deep red clay of Georgia. But the man still lives in me today. I still plow deep furrows and dream of the ocean. I grow seasick with ambition and long to be farming the familiar fields of the heart land again. Somehow, someway, I've got to get life in balance. Dreams and contentment must merge together.

I have few answers for solving this age-old paradox—unless seeing the problem is a big part of the solution. I hope so. For all of us.

Not that I am referring to being in need; for I have learned to be content with whatever I have. I know what it is to have little, and I know what it is to have plenty. In any and all circumstances I have learned the secret of being well-fed and of going hungry, of having plenty and of being in need. I can do all things through him who strengthens me.
PHILIPPIANS 4:11-13

Of course, there is great gain in godliness combined with contentment; for we brought nothing into the world, so that we can take nothing out of it; but if we have food and clothing, we will be content with these.
1 TIMOTHY 6:6-8

Keep your lives free from the love of money, and be content with what you have; for he has said, "I will never leave you, or forsake you."
HEBREWS 13:5-6

A man travels the world over in search of what he needs and returns home to find it.[1]
GEORGE MOORE

An object in possession seldom retains the same charm that it had in pursuit.[2]
PLINY THE YOUNGER

Man struggles to find life outside himself, unaware that the life he is seeking is within him.[3]
KAHLIL GIBRAN

People throw away what they could have by insisting on perfection, which they cannot have, and looking for it where they will never find it.[4]
EDITH SCHAEFFER

Use my dreams, O Lord, to form me into your servant. But may I never forget that I, too, have an Achilles' heel. May dreams and ambitions not be the sword that severs my tendon and cripples me. May I learn the wisdom of contentment amidst challenge, of growth amidst stability.

Grant that I might love both the field and the ocean, yet seek not to possess either. Help me to understand that the greatest things in life are free, your gift of grace to all who follow you. Amen.

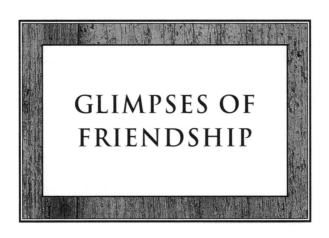

GLIMPSES OF
FRIENDSHIP

SAVING
THE PAST

SPRING CLEANING MANIA HAD GOTTEN
hold of me. Working past midnight in my office, I had at last
cleared my cluttered desk and was now turning to confront my
bulging filing cabinets. It had been years since I had pruned and
weeded my files. Now, I was running out of storage space. I
needed to spend the bucks to buy more filing cabinets or throw
some old and outdated files away.

Because it was late and I wanted to attack something easy, I
turned to my address file and began to thumb through the dog-
eared index cards. Some of the names seemed as if they belonged
to people in another life. High school buddies, college friends,
seminary colleagues, families from my first pastorate in Kentucky—each card sparked a memory from years, indeed decades,
gone by. Every other card bore an address that I knew was no
longer correct and so I began to flip old cards into the trash can.

I had made my way through the "W"s when I came across
the name of Laura Williams. Now, that made me sit back and
think. The address was twenty years old and obviously not current, but the memory was fresh and clear.

I had met Laura when I was twenty-two and she was twenty.
Recently graduated from college, I was touring the nation
singing with a music group. We were playing college concerts and
hitting three campuses a week. And that's when Laura hit me.

We were in Tennessee when I first saw her. A blind man
couldn't miss her. Tall, brunette, with a radiant smile, she was

beautiful. I was on her campus for two days, just long enough to become totally infatuated, and then it was time to move on. Laura and I wrote a lot, ran up a phone bill, and saw each other a few more times. But it's one of those stories that almost everyone shares. Boy meets girl, and the chemistry seems right. But time moves on, distance grows greater, letters grow fewer, and sometime later you hear that she's married and you're married, and a lovely human being becomes an address card lost in a file.

Cherishing the memory but not needing an incorrect address, I let Laura's card fall in the trash can. As I stood to leave, I yawned, turned off the light, and stared into darkness. My thoughts lingered with Laura.

I wonder where she is now? What she looks like? Who she married? I bet she has a dozen kids and has totally forgotten who I am. I wonder if I wrote her if she'd even remember? Of course, she would. I think. Maybe not. I don't even have her current address.

Suddenly I hesitated, "If I throw that card away, that's it. I'll lose track of her, lose the only tie to that part of the past."

Flicking the light back on, I rummaged through the overflowing trash can until I found Laura's card. Placing it in the middle of my spotless desk, I called it a night and drove home, smiling at a pleasant memory come to life.

The next morning as I sat down to work, the address card greeted me. I knew what I needed to do. I called the university Laura attended and asked for the alumni office. Within three minutes I knew her married name, where she lived, and that she had three children. I was pleased.

Picking up the phone, I called her. With the sound of her surprised but delighted voice, twenty years melted away. Filled with laughter and warmth, we talked for fifteen minutes. We now write or call once every year or two and send Christmas cards. But we almost lost it. I almost threw it away. If I had discarded the address card, not made the phone call, all that would have been left was a fading memory.

What I'm reflecting on is not an old boyfriend/girlfriend flare-up. Since my spring cleaning fling, I've also called my best friend from junior high, a buddy on my college soccer team, a favorite professor, and many other long lost friends. Getting in touch with Laura connected me with something of great importance: if we're not careful, we can lose a lot of people who have meant much to us. It's easy to trash the past and lose the richness of our life.

I am writing this chapter at a friend's beach house in Charleston, South Carolina. For seven years I was the pastor of a church in Charleston before moving to Texas. Several days ago I flew back to Charleston for vacation and retreat and rented a car, impatient to ride around the streets of one of the loveliest cities in the world.

Rolling down the windows, I breathed deeply the warm salt air and began to absorb the lovely ambiance of old colonial homes stained with the lineage of history. Spontaneously I thanked the Lord for beautiful memories and for the privilege of having lived in this wonderful city. It is a true gift to be able to relish returning to a place of fondness.

Yet, within an hour, I began to feel lonely. The city still held its beauty and charm, but there was a profound emptiness. I realized that what I was missing was the people who made Charleston special for me. As Adam was afflicted while alone in the beautiful Garden of Eden, I felt a sense of melancholy and discomfort. I began to yearn to visit old neighbors, telephone friends, make plans to meet people for dinner. Charleston is an enchanting place to visit, yes! But the charm quickly dissipates without friends to share it with.

And so is life. We travel from place to place. People come and go. We make new friends in every port. But, if we do not nurture the friendships of the past, we become people who squander our inheritance, who let the true richness of life dribble through our parted fingers. And we discover that we have an address book full of old names but a heart that is lonely.

Not long ago, a major psychological study was completed in which the lives of hundreds of Harvard graduates were carefully monitored and analyzed for thirty years. One of the dominant findings was that the Harvard graduates who became the most successful, happy, and emotionally balanced were people whose lives were characterized by sustained and enduring relationships. Long-term stability was not caused by lack of trauma, failure, or bad luck. Rather, emotional stability and personal success was built on a foundation of meaningful and maintained relationships.

One of my favorite writers and humorists was the late Lewis Grizzard. Tragically, Lewis died after an extended struggle with heart disease. Life has not been the same for me or any other Georgia bulldog fan without his downhome redneck humor. I really miss old Grizzard. No one can take his place.

Yesterday I was in a bookstore and was leafing through the pages of Lewis's final book. Though laced with humor, it is unusually serious. In the final chapter Grizzard lists twenty lessons that he learned from his illness and how he hoped these insights would change his life. A few of them I can't repeat in this book or in polite company, but one of them I can. Lewis simply said that there are a lot of people from his past whom he loved dearly and would make a commitment to call at least once a year.

When we're ready to leave this world, all that really matters is those whom we have loved and who have loved us. But now there is still time to love them, call them, touch them, hug them, and thank them. It might cause us to live a little longer. And for sure it will help us live deeper, richer, and happier lives.

A suggestion: Flip through your old address card file. But don't throw the cards away. Just update them. Make them current. There is no sense in trashing the beauty of the past and losing the sweetness of some of the greatest friendships you will ever have. For as Sophocles said centuries ago, "To throw away an honest friend is as it were, to throw your life away."

A friend loves at all times, and kinsfolk are born to share adversity.
PROVERBS 17:17

Do not abandon old friends, for new ones cannot equal them.
ECCLESIASTICUS 9:10

Perhaps we instinctively know that when we come to the bottom line in life it's not money, career, fame, a fine house, land, or material possessions that are important—it is the people in our lives who love and care for us. People in our lives who are committed to us and on whom we count for support and help are what really matter.[1]
NICK STINNETT

Go oft to the house of thy friend, for weeds choke the unused path.[2]
RALPH WALDO EMERSON

It takes a long time to grow an old friend.[3]
JOHN LEONARD

A doctor wrote a letter of thanks to a schoolteacher for having given him so much encouragement when he had been in her class 30 years before. He later received this reply: "I want you to know what your note meant to me. I am an old lady in my eighties, living alone in a small room, cooking my own meals, lonely, and seeming like the last leaf on the tree. You will be interested to know that I taught school for fifty years and yours is the first letter of appreciation I have ever received. It came on a cold, blue

morning and cheered my lonely old heart as nothing has cheered me in many years.[4]
MARTIN BUXBAUM

Dear Lord, thank you for filling my life with wonderful friends. As time progresses, new chapters are written, and people come and go, it is easy to get out of touch. Father, may I not let friendship die. May I understand that relationships in my past are the greatest treasure for the present day. May I be faithful to water the garden of friendship. Amen.

BEST
FRIENDS

VIC GREENE AND I HAVE BEEN CLOSE friends since we were eleven years old and our parents were missionaries in the Philippines.

I can still picture the first time I met him. Tall and childishly handsome, he moved as if he had coiled springs for legs. He sported an athletic crew cut, wore a sweatshirt, blue jeans and sneakers, and was cradling a scuffed-up football as if it were his identity badge. With pride he told me that back in the States he had been quarterback on his youth league football team. I was impressed and more than a little intimidated. This was a guy worth getting to know.

As we grew older, we became what we called best friends, an important distinction for young teenagers. We learned to play basketball together; we were bunk mates at summer camps; and we went through the agony and ecstacy of discovering girls together.

Unfortunately, though, we each discovered the same girl. She was a whiz at playing one of us against the other, but somehow it never dented our friendship. It probably helped that soon after this mutual romance erupted, I was shipped off to the States when my Dad developed serious health problems. Vic won the girlfriend and got more than he or I could handle.

A few months later my Dad died, and Vic and I didn't see each other for four years during high school. However, we wrote a lot of hastily scrawled letters on thin airmail stationery that crisscrossed the Pacific. Somewhere in the process we pledged to each other that we would attend the same college.

Vic received an academic scholarship to Furman University, and I tagged along, far more interested in soccer, music, parties, and girls than I was in academics. My grades reflected my priorities, and Vic nursed me through our freshman year.

Late at night in our dorm, while Vic was hitting the books hard, I would retreat to a far off corner completely absorbed in writing poetry and short stories. I wouldn't let anybody read my stuff except Vic. He alone was worthy of my trust and the intimacy of my thoughts. Vic was a lot kinder than my literature teacher and in his own way encouraged me to keep writing. As time passed, we became far more like brothers than friends.

Upon college graduation, I spent a wild year touring with a music group while Vic dutifully waited for his college sweetheart to finish school. When he told me that he was going to marry Allison, I couldn't believe it. Didn't want to believe it. But soon I was singing in his wedding and time was moving on. Little did I know that before a year had passed, I would fall in love with Beth, and Vic would be a groomsman in my wedding.

Independently of each other, we decided to enter the ministry, attended the same seminary, and were both called to our first churches in Georgia. And even though we have lived apart for the last ten years, we have remained close. It seems that we will always walk through life together.

Once our children were out of diapers, Vic and I decided to start a family tradition that would help our kids to also know each other. So each November we come together for an energetic weekend of camping in the mountains. We have shared some wonderful moments of introducing our boys to hiking, pitching tents, and telling ghost stories around the camp fire. As our children grow older, we are going to have to find a bigger tent!

One year I loaded my sons, Drew and Luke, in our van and drove from seaside Charleston to mountainous Greenville, South Carolina, to meet Vic for the annual campout. Arriving at his house after dark, we put our sleepy children to bed and felt the house grow sane and quiet. In his den, we sat down by a roaring fire.

I had been looking forward to this time of conversation for weeks. Yet, now as we sat by the hearth and engaged in small talk, I began to grow uneasy. I felt as if I wanted to say something profound, to dredge up the depth of my soul and let this life long companion hear the rhythm and struggles of my heart. But words failed me. I didn't know what to say, where to begin, and so we sat for a few moments in silence.

Finally, I blurted, "I don't know how to ask a question big enough or say something deep enough. The words won't come." He smiled and shook his head. He knew what I was talking about. Again we lapsed into silence. But now it was not uncomfortable. Now it was the silence of the communion of friends.

Best friends are people with whom you can really talk. But best friends are also people with whom you can be quiet for hours and share in the beauty of solitude. Perhaps more important, best friends are folks whose simple *presence* is more important than their words.

As a pastor, I am slowly growing to understand the importance of the word *presence*. In my early years, I used to get nervous when visiting the critically ill or scenes of trauma or crisis. I felt as if I was expected to *do something*: say the right thing, pray the right prayer, be the right person for that moment. But gratefully I have come to see that one's task is not so much to say or do anything but rather to be keenly and faithfully *present*.

I have come to understand that, as Christians, we each symbolically represent the presence of God to one another. For instance, when people drop by to talk to me about their struggles, I certainly don't have all the answers and frequently lack wisdom. But somehow through sharing together, they come to feel that a third party is present, the very presence of God. We can lead people into the presence of God simply by being with them, talking with them, suffering with them, supporting them.

88   There is something holy about sitting in silence by a fireside
with a good and enduring friend. It is an experience different
from worship. But somehow the presence of someone bigger,
someone ultimate, is felt. There is a feeling of being at home, of
being connected through friendship to a Source that is grander
than human minds can comprehend. Friendship is a catalyst
that can lead to an awareness of the presence of God.

And so, do such fireside moments come frequently? No, they
don't. And are such friendships rare? Yes, they are, and worth
their weight in gold. Best friends are one of the spiritual treasures of life that are priceless but available to all.

Don't take your best friends for granted. Celebrate your history. Let them know that more than their words and humor,
their very self is important to you. Their warm presence will cut
the chill on many a winter night.

*When David had finished speaking to Saul, the soul of
Jonathan was bound to the soul of David, and Jonathan
loved him as his own soul.*
    1 SAMUEL 18:1

*Now a certain man was ill, Lazarus of Bethany, of the vil-
lage of Mary and her sister Martha. . . . When Jesus
arrived, he found that Lazarus had already been in the
tomb four days. . . . When Mary came where Jesus was and
saw him, she knelt at his feet and said to him, "Lord, if you
had been here, my brother would not have died." When
Jesus saw her weeping, and the Jews who came with her,
also weeping, he was greatly disturbed in spirit and deeply
moved. . . . Jesus began to weep. So the Jews said, "See how
he loved him!"*
    JOHN 11:1, 17, 32-33, 35-36

For where two or three are gathered in my name, I am
there among them.
MATTHEW 18:20

Faithful friends are life-saving medicine.
ECCLESIASTICUS 6:16

*Friendship is the inexpressible comfort of feeling safe with
a person having neither to weigh thoughts nor measure
words.*[1]
GEORGE ELIOT

*It is one of the blessings of old friends that you can afford to
be stupid with them.*[2]
RALPH WALDO EMERSON

*Your friend is the man who knows all about you, and still
likes you.*[3]
ELBERT HUBBARD

*One friend in a lifetime is much, two are many, three are
hardly possible.*[4]
HENRY ADAMS

*We are all of us calling and calling across the incalculable
gulfs which separate us even from our nearest friends.*[5]
DAVID GRAYSON

*We once believed that our friends were our friends only
when our love and trust were absolute, when we shared
identical tastes and passions and goals, when we felt that
we could bare the darkest secrets of our souls with utter
impunity, when we willingly would run—no questions
asked—to help each other in times of trouble. We once
believed that our friends were our friends only when they*

fit that mythic model. But growing up means giving up that view. For even if we are lucky enough to have one or two or three beloved "best friends," friendships, we learn, are at best an imperfect connection. . . .

And yet, despite the ambivalence . . . the fact that friends are friends only in spots, the friendships we create may be as strong, and sometimes stronger, than those we form through flesh and blood and law—comforting and exuberant, "sacred and miraculous" connections.[6]
JUDITH VIORST

Heavenly Father, I often feel so lonely. It is the blight of life. But I know that loneliness is the human condition; that not even your Son, Jesus Christ, escaped its hollow pain.

Father, I give you thanks for my closest friends, scattered throughout the wanderings of my life. Though seldom do we see each other, our souls once merged have never parted.

I confess that our relationships are no more perfect than we as individuals are perfect. But the love of my friends and my love for them is what gives me greatest hope for Heaven.

I have come to believe, O God, that Heaven is not so much a place as it is a relationship, a merging of all that has loved and been loved. Best friends are but a glimpse of what shall be. And for this, I am eternally grateful. Amen.

BITING THE
HAND THAT HELPS

11

I HAVE ALWAYS LOVED ANIMALS, ESPE-
cially dogs. When I don't have a smiling, slobbering retriever to
welcome me home or accompany me on walks, something special is missing in my life.

It is my love for animals that caused me to help start a humane
society some years ago while living in Monroe, North Carolina. I
consider the abuse and neglect of animals to be a spiritual problem that calls for responsible action by Christians. However, I
never dreamed I'd get mixed up in so many tense situations.

I remember one particular morning when our bedside
phone rang at dawn. Thinking it was the alarm clock, I flailed at
the snooze button until Beth handed me the receiver. Half
awake, I heard a hysterical lady scream, "I just hit a dog! The
police told me to call you. He's still alive and I'm scared to touch
him. He's in front of Hill Top Restaurant. Please hurry!" The
phone went dead.

Pulling on my blue jeans, I knew that this Monday was starting off sideways. "Why couldn't the police handle this?" I griped.
"They get paid, not me!"

As I jumped in my van, I realized that traffic would soon be
picking up as people went to work. When I neared the restaurant, I could see cars veering onto the shoulder of the highway to
miss a dark object on the center line. No one was stopping. As
my lights focused on the mound in the road, a dog lifted its
head. "I can't believe it!" I exploded as my fist hit the steering

92   wheel. "Nobody even moved the dog! Just left him there to get hit again."

I parked my van and ran over to the animal, a mixed chow and shepherd, and knelt down as another man stopped to help. While he directed traffic, I visually inspected the dog without touching him. There were no head injuries. His back did not seem to be broken. He wasn't paralyzed. But it didn't take a veterinarian to see the jagged bone sticking out of one of his rear legs. His pelvis was also probably fractured.

Running back to my van, I opened the door and grabbed the gear I kept for such emergencies: a pair of thick leather gloves, a rope muzzle, adhesive tape, and a wide board. From here on, things could get tricky.

As I jerked on my gloves, I tried to figure out how to best slide the dog onto the board without hurting him or losing an arm. When I reached to touch him, he snarled in fear and pain. This was not going to be easy.

As a lady knelt in front of the dog and attracted his attention, I moved behind the chow to try and loop the muzzle over his nose. Never coordinated, I missed his square nose but the dog did not miss me. As he crunched down on my descending hand, I felt raw pain shoot up my arm. Somehow in the process, however, I was able to grab the dog's snout and hold it shut as he released my hand, the glove still in his mouth. Quickly we restrained the panicked animal and slid him gently onto the board. Several bystanders picked the board up and placed the dog in the back of my van.

En route to the emergency animal clinic, my hand turned numb and then throbbing pain crept in. Thanks to the thick gloves, the skin was not cut. But it felt as if a bone was crushed. Fortunately, this was not the case. All that was wounded was my pride. But I had once again learned a classic lesson: "A wounded animal will bite the hand that helps him." I have thought of this maxim many times since that morning as I have dealt not so much with injured dogs, but with hurting people.

All of us have friends whom we love and care for who get 93
run over and injured by events in life. Many are left alone on life's
highway, paralyzed and in pain. Responding to their plight and
need is often difficult.

Sometimes our reaction is a relatively easy matter when a
friend's house burns down or they are recovering from surgery.
Most of us can respond well to such overt and public situations.
But it is the more subtle, yet no less difficult, injuries that leave us
perplexed as to what role, if any, we should play.

What do you say to a friend when it is rumored that her
marriage is on the rocks or that she and her husband might be
separating? How do you respond when you know that some of
your closest friends have learned that their son is homosexual
and has contracted AIDS? How do you react when it has just
become public knowledge that a close friend has been having an
affair or has lost a job due to alleged incompetency, malpractice,
or dishonesty. Situations such as these are ones that leave us sitting on the edge of our bed in the early morning, shaking our
bleary heads, wondering how in the world we should respond, or
if we should respond at all.

In the story I have related of the injured dog, I have caught a
glimpse into an analogy of truth that has helped me. I think this
insight can be seen in several ways.

(1) The Decision. When friends are hurting, we do have a choice
as to whether or not we will respond. Just as I sat on the edge of
the bed on that early morning and made an unpleasant decision
to rescue a dog, so must we decide if we will take action to help a
friend in need. Such decisions are often difficult and complex.
They are seldom convenient. And they throw us into a state of
reluctance and hesitation. However, allow me to make a bold
statement. I have come to believe that to be Christlike, we usually
have no choice. We must respond in some manner.

If I understand correctly Jesus' parable of the Good Samaritan, every traveler on the road saw the beaten and injured man

and knew he was in need. However, only the Samaritan decided to help. Thus develops the theme of the parable: Christians are people who are compelled to respond to the need of friends—even strangers and enemies—if they are to live within the ethic of the kingdom of God. How we respond is debatable. When we respond is optional. But that we respond is imperative. It is the imperative of Christian love.

(2) The Approach. Having decided to respond to the need of a hurting friend, however, the approach one takes to help is entirely another matter. This is where things become difficult.

No self-help book can be written to cover every situation to which you will be asked to respond. Not only is each situation different, but each person involved in the situation is different. Some dogs in pain will bite you, and some dogs won't. Some people are willing to talk about their problems, and some will not. Some friends welcome help, and some resist. It is not an easy task to decide how to place a wounded friend on a stretcher so that you can help carry her in her hour of need.

Yet, the moment comes when you must try something. You cannot stand in the middle of the road forever. You have to grab hold of the situation in the best way that you can and take your chances.

Sometimes nothing short of a personal visit or a to-the-point conversation will do. Many situations can best be addressed by a sensitive letter or a supportive phone call. Other times words do not need to be spoken, just simple personal presence is enough. The decision of how to respond is no exact science, not even an intuitive art. Sometimes it is a shot in the dark. But that we must respond is unavoidable.

(3) The Helper. For the Christian, there is a wonderful resource available to us when we commit ourselves to respond to another's need. Jesus calls the resource "the Helper," or the Holy Spirit (John 14: 14-18; 26).

Many times I have stood at a hospital door and before knocking have prayed, "Lord, I don't know what I'm doing here. I don't know what to say or how to say it. I don't even want to be here. Please speak through me. I've got to depend on you."

At other times I have sat down to lunch with a friend whose life has fallen apart and I have whispered silently, "God, you take charge of this conversation. I don't know how in the world we are going to talk about what we need to talk about. I'm going to relax and let you handle this situation."

The amazing thing is that when we make ourselves available to help others, the Spirit of God becomes our Helper. Somehow God's Spirit finds a way for us to express what needs to be expressed—a word, a hug, a look, a memory, a joke, tears and laughter. God is with us. He leads; we follow. If this were not true, I would not have the courage to minister to the needs of others. I would mind my own business and stay home.

(4) The Danger. As with the dog that bit me, there is danger and risk involved when we try to help. Granted, most animals have not snapped at me when I have stopped to help, but all of them have looked at me with eyes of fear, distrust, and concern. It is not a comfortable time. And it is no different with human beings.

In times of crisis, many people are simply not themselves. Grief, fear, and pain elicit from all of us irrational responses. Physically we are depleted. Our patience wears thin. Frequently we grow paranoid and suspect everyone. We become increasingly angry and frustrated, and lash out. And often the person who receives our anger is an innocent bystander or a friend whom we care for dearly. It seems that it is those whom we love and trust the most who often receive the fury of our most primal feelings. It is often ugly. It is not pleasant But it is real.

If in helping we are the one whose hand is bitten, we can remember that we are not trying to lend support in order to be thanked, understood, or to feel good about our service. We can place a thick glove of objectivity around our exposed feelings and remember that we are there for only one reason—to try and aid the other person. Whether they accept our help or are thankful is beyond our control. And, for a while, it must be beyond our concern.

Perhaps one of the most frustrating moments in rescuing an injured animal is when in their fear they run away from their very source of help. Many times I have tried to coax a wounded dog or cat out of the woods or have slowly tried to approach them. It is heartbreaking to see them cower and run limping away to die a slow death or be maimed for life. And yet, you cannot control this factor. Whether or not an animal or a friend chooses to accept your help and friendship is beyond your power. You can only do your best to offer your aid and support. But this one thing you must do. You must make the attempt, take the initiative, risk rejection, and trust the good Lord to show you the way.

(5) The Result. My dog story has a happy ending. Old Rover— actually named "Hill Top"—had some tough and trying days. The X-rays revealed that he had two broken legs and a cracked pelvis. Fortunately, no joints were crushed. The big decision was whether or not to put the dog to sleep. I decided that if he stabilized, I would bring him home and we would take things a day at a time.

Again, I didn't know what I was getting into. The first few weeks Hill Top required constant time and care from my family. However, the little chow gradually mended and got better. He'll always have a limp and, I hope, a healthy fear of cars. But today Hill Top's got a good home on a farm in North Carolina.

The final memory I have of the dog was when I drove him out to meet his adoption family. I let him out of the car and he was immediately besieged by three children wanting to pet him. I picked him up, stroked his ears one last time, and I kid you not, Hill Top licked my hand, the same hand he had bitten six months before. It was a happy and tearful moment.

And so it is when we serve in the name of Christ. Usually our friends who snap and bite when they are hurt will in time come around to love us in their own unique way. It usually takes a lot of time and a lot of prayer. And it requires more love than any of us have. But the Helper never runs out. The Holy Spirit continues to love. The Spirit is willing to be bitten again and again.

Sometimes the hardest task in life is to love a friend. But a friendship without pain and struggle is a friendship that is usually shallow. Most of my closest friends have bitten me many times. And you can be doggone sure, I've bitten them back!

Jesus replied, "A man was going down from Jerusalem to Jericho, and fell into the hands of robbers, who stripped him, beat him, and went away, leaving him half dead. . . . But a Samaritan while traveling came near him; and when he saw him, he was moved with pity. He went to him and bandaged his wounds, having poured oil and wine on them. Then he put him on his own animal, brought him to an inn, and took care of him. The next day he took out two denarii, gave them to the innkeeper, and said, 'Take care of him; and when I come back, I will repay you whatever more you spend.'"
LUKE 10:30, 33-35

Then the king will say . . . "I was hungry and you gave me food, I was thirsty and you gave me something to drink, I was a stranger and you welcomed me, I was naked and you gave me clothing, I was sick and you took care of me, I was in prison and you visited me."

Then the righteous will answer him, "Lord, when was it that we saw you hungry and gave you food, or thirsty and gave you something to drink? And when was it that we saw you a stranger and welcomed you, or naked and gave

98

you clothing? And when was it that we saw you sick or in prison and visited you?" And the king will answer them, "Truly I tell you, just as you did it to one of the least of these who are members of my family, you did it to me."
MATTHEW 25:34-40

Bear one another's burdens, and in this way you will fulfill the law of Christ.
GALATIANS 6:2

Love anything and your heart will be wrung and possibly broken. If you want to make sure of keeping it intact you must give it to no one, not even an animal. Wrap it carefully round with hobbies and little luxuries; avoid all entanglements. Lock it up safe in the casket or coffin of your selfishness. But in that casket—safe, dark, motionless, airless—it will change. It will not be broken; it will become unbreakable; impenetrable, irredeemable. To love is to be vulnerable.[1]
C. S. LEWIS

To build a relationship, be it with God, a spouse or whomever, means to [experience] hurt, struggle, and risk. It means opening up all sides of us . . . I am convinced that often the tougher the struggle in working out a relationship the greater the eventual satisfaction.[2]
DONALD W. FRY

If we could read the secret history of our enemies, we should find in each man's life sorrow and suffering enough to disarm all hostility.[3]
HENRY WADSWORTH LONGFELLOW

The art of being wise is the art of knowing what to overlook.[4]
WILLIAM JAMES

The most I can do for my friend is simply to be his friend.[5]
HENRY DAVID THOREAU

Dear God, people see me as gregarious, but you know I'm shy. I can sound tough, but I'll walk a country mile to avoid conflict. To take the initiative to talk with a friend about a problem they are having turns my stomach into knots. It's easier to mind my own business, plead ignorance, flash a hide-behind smile.

But Lord, I know that Christian love is expressed by taking the initiative, by stopping to help and not leaving the task for someone else. I guess I'm a reluctant Good Samaritan. I know what I want to do, need to do. But I lack courage and skill.

Father, help me to see that courage and skill is your job; that you will provide—and that stopping to be present is my job. Help me to extend my hand to others and not to fear the consequence. Amen.

UNKNOWN FRIENDS

I WAS YOUNG, TOO YOUNG TO THINK abstractly. However, I was keenly connected to my feelings. As a six year old I knew that something momentous was happening. I was both excited and frightened.

My feet were vibrating on the shuddering deck beneath me. Crowded against a tall life-rail, I looked between iron bars into a sea of faces far below. I reached up and anxiously grasped my father's large hand. As I gazed into his tanned face for reassurance, he smiled at me. Yet, I could sense that he was also nervous. This was a time of destiny in his life. His grin was pinched and tight.

The year was 1957 and the place was San Francisco harbor. We were standing on the deck of an American President Liner, the *S.S. President Wilson*, departing for the Philippine Islands, where my parents would be missionaries. Three weeks on a passenger liner sailing across the balmy Pacific would be great fun, but now the reality of leaving one's homeland with two young children bore down on my father and mother.

As the hawser lines were cast away and the *President Wilson* slowly thrust herself away from the dock, the deck crew distributed small rolls of colored paper to the passengers. I remember thinking that the paper looked like large rolls of caps for my Lone Ranger cap pistol, but my father told me that they were something called streamers.

I watched as passengers held on to one end of the streamers and threw the brightly colored ribbons toward the people gathered on the pier below. Some of the women in the crowd were wives of the ship's crew come to wish them *bon voyage*. Others were relatives and friends of passengers. People began to laugh and cheer as a loved one caught the other end of a streamer, symbol of one last and final touch. Soon there was a rainbow of bright streamers draped between the pier and the slowly departing ocean liner.

We did not have friends or relatives on the pier. However, it did not matter to me. I took a streamer with my small hands and hurled it overboard. I was surprised and delighted when a young woman caught the other end and waved to me.

Though this moment was thirty-eight years ago, I vividly remember this unknown woman. She was tall with thick brunette hair flowing to her shoulders. I could not see her eyes, but she had broad, high cheek bones and a radiant, contagious smile, outlined by lipstick. Her body was slender, shrouded by a long tan coat to cut the cold ocean breeze. She wore high heels and had a leather purse draped over her shoulder. She was a picture of beauty for me, an instant and innocent crush for a six year old.

She waved excitedly, and my father and I waved back. Dad shouted something to her, words I do not remember. I could see her mouth move as she answered, her words lost in the throb of diesel engines and the noise of the crowd. By now the *President Wilson* was gliding away from the dock, moving ever faster down the length of the pier. As distance increased, the streamers began to tighten and tear, blowing wildly in the breeze as the ship edged farther away.

When my red streamer grew taught and neared the breaking point, the young woman walked quickly down the pier following the ship, not allowing the streamer to grow fully extended. As the ship gained speed she began to run until she stopped at the very end of the pier. Waving as the streamer finally snapped, she playfully blew me a kiss and I blew one back. Slowly she faded from view but never from memory. In my mind tonight, she stands at the end of that pier as beautiful and vibrant as ever. She has never let go of the streamer.

There are so many people in my life who have never let go of the streamer. And all of them are strangers, people I have not met or spoken to, many whose faces I have only seen in old black-and-white pictures. Most of these friends were introduced through books.

I think of Albert Schweitzer. He was dead before I ever heard his name, but he has shaped my life. As a college student, I learned of how Schweitzer became a world renowned theologian/philosopher and lectured throughout Europe and the United States. He was also a popular concert organist and an authority on the music of Johann Sebastian Bach. By age thirty-eight he had the world at his feet. But at this same age, he left the ivory towers and concert halls of Europe and went to medical school. Upon graduation, he departed for equatorial Africa to build a hospital and spend the rest of his life ministering to the poor.

I never met Schweitzer. But I know him. He stands on the pier and holds onto a streamer that I grasp with my hands of idealism. He has never let go of that fragile ribbon of relationship. And on dark nights when I examine my life and its purpose, Schweitzer speaks to me. He speaks not so much by words but by example. He has taught me a lot. He needs to teach me more.

There are others who stand on the pier with the lovely young woman who gave me friendship and the white-haired Schweitzer who gave me ideals. I see Elton Trueblood and Leslie Weatherhead; Erich Fromm and Paul Tournier; Emil Brunner and St. Augustine; Frederick Buechner and John Keats. I've never met one of them. They span the centuries. But they all stand on the pier and hold a streamer grasped by my mind, thoughts, dreams, and imagination. They are friends and mentors. They share my most private moments, my deepest introspection, the formulation of my hopes and dreams. And some of the best conversations I have ever known have been with these great people.

Yes, when I think of friendship, I must think of the living and the dead. And I must also remember those who by God's grace have reached out and grasped a colorful streamer thrown out by the hand of a child. What would my life be without these people who stand on the pier and wish me *bon voyage*? What would life be without the beautiful smile of a woman whose name I will never know, her kiss blown sweetly forever? And how could I navigate the seas of life without the saintly specter of a Schweitzer always pointing to a better and higher way? I thank God for unknown friends.

I thank my God every time I remember you.
PHILIPPIANS 1:3

Bow down thine ear, and hear the words of the wise and apply thine heart unto knowledge.
PROVERBS 22:17 (KJV)

Be not forgetful to entertain strangers; for thereby some have entertained angels unawares.
HEBREW 13:2 (KJV)

The reading of all good books is like conversation with the finest men of past centuries.[1]
RENÉ DESCARTES

A man is known by the company his mind keeps.[2]
THOMAS BAILEY ALDRICH

104

Lives of great men, all remind us
We can make our lives sublime
And departing leave behind us
Footprints in the sands of time.[3]
   HENRY WADSWORTH LONGFELLOW

A teacher affects eternity; he can never tell where his influence stops.[4]
   HENRY ADAMS

Example is not the main thing in influencing others. It is the only thing.[5]
   ALBERT SCHWEITZER

Dear God, you have blessed my life with strangers, people I have never met, but who have befriended me. Thank you for their acts of love, their fine example. Thank you for their words written in the silence of the night which echo in the sanctuary of my heart.

May I in turn be a mentor, a friend, to others. May I grasp the bright streamer of a child and send her on her voyage of discovery. Grant that in your kingdom where there are no strangers, we may be united one and all. Amen.

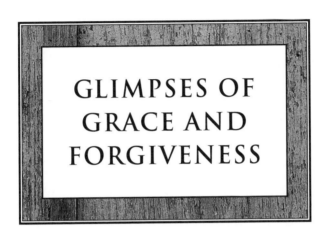

GLIMPSES OF
GRACE AND
FORGIVENESS

THE IRONY
OF GRACE

IT HAD BEEN A HECTIC DAY. BETH AND I were scurrying around trying to get away for a weekend trip. I had been invited to participate in the graduation ceremony at my alma mater, Mercer University, and we were looking forward to a few days of fond college memories.

Rushing to the bank on my way home from the office, I withdrew some money for our trip and was walking back to the car when I first heard his slurred voice. "Hey, man! I'm hungry! How about helping me get some lunch?" Looking around, I saw a young man whom I had frequently seen at the city shelter for the homeless.

His name was Johnny. He had obviously been drinking and was feeling no pain. Being a pastor, I was inured to the antics of con men and drunks, and I did not want to contribute money to this fellow's alcoholism. Tucking my billfold in my pants pocket, I brushed on by him mumbling more to myself than to him.

Halfway down the block Johnny's words caught up with me. I hadn't really heard him, so enmeshed was I in my own affairs. All that he had said was, "I'm hungry." And I had walked on by.

I stopped. For some reason I thought of my father, always a compassionate but realistic man. I asked, "What would Dad have done?" Well, I knew what he would have done. He wouldn't have been in such a hurry. And he would have fed the man.

Turning around, I walked back to Johnny, now hustling someone else coming out of the bank. With a firm look that

108   suggested, "You're not gonna pull one over on me, Fella," I said, "If you're hungry, Johnny, I'll buy your lunch, but I'm not giving you any money. Is that a deal?"

I could see the hesitation in his eyes. My offer was not the best he could have hoped for—but it was not the worst, either. Johnny grinned through broken, rotten teeth and said, "Sounds like a deal to me."

We were standing in front of a restaurant. Nodding toward the door I said, "This looks like a good place, lets go." Shuffling behind me and looking uncomfortable among the neatly dressed business people milling in and out, Johnny followed me over to the manager at the cash register.

"My friend needs a meal," I said with a subtle wink. "If I give you five dollars, do you think that would cover lunch?"

"Sure," the man said with a smile that answered my wink. "We can come up with something good for five dollars."

Handing the cashier a crisp bill from the bank, I turned to tell Johnny to order what he wanted. It was then that he hit me with the big question: "Hey, man, if I don't eat that much can I keep the change?"

Like a father answering a two year old I replied, "I don't think so, Johnny. We're not playing that game. You get what you want to eat and that's as far as it goes."

Walking with Johnny to a table, I saw that he was seated and then I left. I had made the best of a bad situation, I thought. Feeling good about my actions, I hurried home to load the car, pick up Beth, and get out of town.

As Charleston faded away and we sped down the highway, I mentioned my good deed for the day to Beth and promptly forgot about Johnny. I was busy thinking about the events ahead.

If I'm honest, I was nervous. The president of my alma mater had asked me to present an academic hood to an old family friend who was receiving an honorary doctorate from the university. I was delighted to do this. Yet I also felt apprehensive. What if I flubbed up? What if I dropped the hood or draped it around the man's glasses or did something embarrassing? As the miles sped by, I tried to reassure myself that mine was an easy task.

The next morning as Beth and I dressed for the graduation exercises, I felt the butterflies beginning to return. We had over-slept and not allowed time to eat breakfast. Knowing that I could not make it through the long graduation without something to eat, I decided to rush out and quickly buy some breakfast food. Remembering a donut shop a few blocks away, I told Beth I would make a mad dash and pick her up in ten minutes.

At the donut shop, a pretty young woman greeted me. With a pleasant smile she took my order. As she filled a box with a half-dozen donuts and poured two large cups of steaming coffee, I found myself thinking about Johnny. I wondered what he was doing? Was he sober? I even wondered what he ate for lunch.

Suddenly the young waitress's pleasant voice broke through my thoughts. "That'll be three dollars and fifteen cents," she said as she handed me the bag of donuts. Reaching in my pocket for my billfold, I suddenly froze. My billfold was not there. With a rising sense of panic, I remembered seeing it laying on the dresser back at the motel. My mind went blank. "What am I going to do?" I frantically thought as I looked into this young woman's eyes.

Furtively glancing at the people clustered around the counter, I felt my face flush. Grinning sheepishly and speaking in a low voice, I heard myself stammering, "I don't believe this! I left my billfold at the motel. I don't have a cent on me. Could I possibly come back and pay you this afternoon?"

The young lady smiled at me with a twinkle in her eye that disarmed me. Laughing she said, "You don't need to come back. These donuts will just be on us. Everybody needs a break every once in awhile. You take them and enjoy them."

Several moments later as I drove away in a car filled with the aroma of donuts and coffee, I knew that God had just clobbered me with a big lesson. It was a lesson so great that I couldn't fully grasp it. But through a glimpse, a moment in time, I learned

110   something about the grace of God. I learned primarily that all of us—every one of us—is equally in need of the graciousness of God. Standing there in my suit and tie ready to go to a university graduation, I was no different than ragged Johnny standing half-looped on the sidewalk, asking for a free lunch.

Life has a way of being a great equalizer. And if we think our own virtue and accomplishments will get us anywhere close to the door of heaven, then we haven't lived long enough or deep enough. Sooner or later we will find ourselves reaching for our billfold of earned goodness only to find a pocket full of emptiness. We are totally dependent on the grace of God. Every single one of us! And that is the gospel. The only meal we'll ever eat in heaven is a free one, one that we never paid for or deserved.

I learned something else. God is a lot more like that kind, young waitress than he is like me. She gave to me with a sense of joy and compassion. Her generosity set me free. She understood me and felt for me. There was a sense of delight in her giving, a smile that was authentic and free.

My giving to Johnny was more than paternalistic. I looked down my nose at him and gave out of a sense of condescending obligation. Whatever he felt when I left him in that restaurant, I don't think he felt that I loved him. Cared about him? Maybe. But loved him? Probably not. Somehow my righteous compassion did not give him a glimpse into the love of God. I did not smile. My eyes did not say, "I love you." My giving did not free him up to accept the goodness of life.

Finally, I learned in that donut shop that until we have been helpless and empty and have been freely given to, we are probably not able to give freely to others. To give with joy is to know that you've been there too.

And so it is with forgiveness. Until we have fallen on our own face a time or two and discovered our own bankruptness, it is hard to understand the absolute graciousness of God's forgiveness. But it's true. God is always willing to forgive our sins and send us on our way, coffee and donuts in hand.

I think the woman at the donut store changed my life in a significant way. The next time I meet another Johnny, I hope I'll remember my own empty pocket and blushing face and be a little more compassionate. I still won't give cold cash, but I hope that I will authentically smile. I hope that my eyes will let him know that God truly does love him through me. And maybe my love will reveal to him something about the grace and forgiveness of God.

Standing empty-handed in a donut shop in Georgia, a young woman gave me a glimpse into the smiling grace of God. Much to my delight, I saw that God really does love me. And you.

The steadfast love of the Lord never ceases,
his mercies never come to an end;
they are new every morning;
great is your faithfulness.
LAMENTATIONS 3:22-23

But God, who is rich in mercy, out of the great love with
which he loved us even when we were dead through our
trespasses, made us alive together with Christ. . . . For by
grace you have been saved through faith, and this is not
your own doing; it is the gift of God—not the result of
works, so that no one may boast.
EPHESIANS 2:4-5, 8-9

"Blessed are the merciful, for they will receive mercy."
MATTHEW 5:7

As God's chosen ones, holy and beloved, clothe yourselves
with compassion, kindness, humility, meekness, and
patience.
COLOSSIANS 3:12

The Holy Supper is kept indeed,
In whatso we share with another's need;
Not what we give but what we share,
For the gift without the giver is bare;
Who gives himself with his alms feeds three—
Himself, his hungering neighbour, and Me.[1]
    JAMES RUSSELL LOWELL

God redeems us from the sense of failure and the fear of
failure because He sees us as no human eyes can see us.
Some religions teach that God sees us so clearly that He
knows all our shameful thoughts and nasty secrets. I prefer
to believe that God sees us so clearly that He knows better
than anyone else our wounds and sorrows, the scars on our
hearts from having wanted to do more and do better and
being told by the world that we never would.[2]
    HAROLD KUSHNER

Lord Christ, you remain, unseen, at our side, present like
a poor man who washes the feet of his friends. And we,
to follow in your footsteps, we are here, waiting for you to
suggest signs of sharing to make us into servants of your
Gospel.[3]
    BROTHER ROGER

Dear God, nobody knows better than I do that I have an attitude problem today. I don't feel proud or holy. Quite the opposite. I feel tired, drained, pushed, inadequate, and on edge. The needs of my spouse, my children, my colleagues, my friends, are straight-wired to my soul. I am depleted to the point that I no longer care. And that is the greatest problem, for I do care. I care deeply.

And yet, O Father, when the day is done, perhaps those who long for help most have not been touched. The elderly widow who needs only a short phone call to be reassured that I remember her. The boy who lost his father last week and needs to know that I am there for him. And the beggar on the street. His needs are so deep, so complex, so unsolvable that it would take Jesus Christ to . . .

Jesus Christ. Maybe that's the real issue in all of this. It would take Jesus Christ to make any difference at all.

Lord, I don't even know what I am saying. My words have the ring of glib cliché. But words aside, I know that I am right. I need Christ in my life to make any difference.

Take my guilt and give me your grace. Transform my attitude by the love of your Spirit. And when I see Johnny, help me smile from way down deep. Amen.

SETTING THE PRISONER FREE

I WAS A YOUNG MAN, AN ASSOCIATE pastor fresh out of seminary, and wet behind the ears. Struggling with insecurity, I wondered if I could measure up to many people's expectations, much less, my own.

The moment came at 12:30 A.M. on Ash Wednesday. I had just preached at a community-wide Lenten service in Athens, Georgia. I feared that I had not spoken well, not sounded the trumpet as clearly as I had wished.

The obvious problem was that I was nervous, intimidated out of my mind. Nervous because I was speaking in front of my own pastor, and pastors from five other churches. Nervous because this was the first Lenten message I had ever written or delivered. Today, I don't recall a word spoken or a thought expressed. It was a fleeting moment in time.

What I do remember, however, was that as the sanctuary cleared and people moved to the fellowship hall for lunch, I limped back to the pulpit to gather my Bible and notes. The sanctuary grew silent and lonely. Breathing a mixed sigh of anxiety and relief, I heard my performance-driven conscience demand: "How did I do?"

Interrupted by floor boards creaking under the carpeted aisle, I turned to see an old man with a cane shuffling slowly down the center aisle. He waved at me, signaling that he wanted to talk. Bible in hand, I walked down the steps from the pulpit to meet him.

He had a shock of disheveled white hair and a pleasant face, sharply wrinkled, with smiling blue eyes. He looked jaundiced, and I sensed that his health was not good. As I said hello, he lifted his hand to his throat and opened his mouth to speak. That was when I was shocked out of my self-absorption.

His voice did not come from his mouth. It came from where his hand was touching his throat. It was a raspy, mechanical sound, wind being compressed through a voice prosthesis and amplified. Jarred, I realized he was recovering from throat surgery and that his larynx had been removed. "Probably cancer," I thought. "Probably cigarettes."

As he gurgled forth sound and strained to talk, I grew embarrassed. I could not understand a word that the man was saying. And so I bent my head lower, close to the hole in his throat. This time I grasped his words: "Young man, I want to tell you that you have a fine speaking voice. And, I enjoyed your message."

If he had taken his cane and bashed it over my head I could not have been more stunned. The irony of a man who could not speak, who had lost his own voice, taking the time to tell me that he liked my voice, washed over me like a flash flood. I looked at the old man's wrinkled face, nicotine yellow, and tears flooded my eyes. Putting my arm around his shoulders, I found that I, too, was speechless. I knew that I had just been given a priceless gift of grace.

Affirmation and encouragement are two of the most wonderful and life-affirming forms of love that we can give to one another. We are all insecure, even the most cocky and self-assured. Beneath a thin veneer of composure, each of us wonders if we can pass muster and measure up. When somebody affirms us, even a total stranger, suddenly we are enabled to believe more in ourselves. Grace is given to us through kind and supportive words. For grace is the assurance that we are accepted and affirmed for who we are.

116   As I look back over the chapters of my life, I have been blessed to know people who encouraged and affirmed me. I remember a neighbor, Madeline Monroe, who was a voice teacher and heard me shyly humming a tune one day. She asked me to sing for her, and I was absolutely mortified. My sixteen-year-old voice was not sure whether it was baritone or tenor. And I was scared to death to sing in public. Yet, as she began to play the piano in her living room, I sang along louder and louder until I forgot my embarrassment. Suddenly Mrs. Monroe turned and said, "You can really sing! And I want to teach you how."

Teach me she did and started me off on eight years of voice lessons. I never became an opera star or made it to Broadway, but Mrs. Monroe's words of grace set me free to believe that I really could sing. I have been singing and bellowing away ever since. Music has become one of the greatest treasures of my life.

I also remember Dr. Bill Hale. When I met him as the new associate pastor of his church, he saw a vulnerable young man and took me under his wing. An expert communicator and professional speaker, Bill decided to whip a rookie into shape.

In his wisdom, Bill helped form me not by words of criticism but by thoughts of encouragement. Each time that I preached, Bill would invite me by his office the next week for a cup of coffee and a lively postmortem of my sermon. Carving out time in his busy schedule, he would engage with my thoughts, aggressively debate issues, all the time letting me know that as an older man, he was taking me seriously. On occasion Bill recommended another presentation format for my sermon or suggested a different style of introduction or conclusion. But above all he consistently communicated to me the message, "I believe in you! You can preach! Speak with confidence!"

Six years later a more secure associate pastor left Athens, Georgia, to accept his first senior pastorate. Bill Hale went with me in spirit and has been with me ever since. His support and affirmation has given me the en-*courage*-ment to believe that God can speak through me.

Sometimes I wonder what my life would be like if Madeline Monroe and Bill Hale had not reached down and grabbed me by the scruff of the neck. What if they had not seized the moment and challenged me to grow and hone my abilities? Without them I doubt that I would be a pastor today or writing these words tonight. My life would be far less enjoyable and productive if they had not given me the gift of their affirmation and encouragement.

God's grace is frequently imparted to us through the bolstering words of other people. For this reason I believe that every Christian is called to the ministry of graciousness. We are called to "lift up the down trodden and set the prisoner free" by speaking words that build up, fortify, and support. For it is through our voices that people will come to either believe in themselves and contribute positively to life or else doubt themselves and give up on living.

More than twenty years ago a mute old man took the time to tell me that he liked my voice and message. I never learned his name and have not seen him since. He walked into my life in silence and quickly disappeared. But his strengthening words have never stopped ringing in my ears.

On those Sundays when I stand in the pulpit and doubt my ability to bring God's word, I look out and see the old man hobbling down the church aisle, touching his throat and beckoning to me to listen. I also hear Bill Hale's voice declare, "You can do it, boy! You can preach!" In those moments God's grace touches me and I am freed to speak a word of encouragement unto others. For we all must be about a ministry of gracious affirmation, of setting prisoners free.

Death and life are in the power of the tongue. . . .
PROVERBS 18:21

We have gifts that differ according to the grace given to us, let each experience them accordingly. . . . If [a person's gift] is encouraging, let him encourage.
ROMANS 12:6, 8

And let us consider how to provoke one another to love and good deeds, not neglecting to meet together, as is the habit of some, but encouraging one another. . . .
HEBREWS 10:24-25

How many great artrists would have never become so without an obscure master, whose name history has forgotten? The confidence shown in them by their master, quite as much as his teaching, has helped them give of their best.[1]
PAUL TOURNIER

It takes the gift of blessing [from others] to help us know who we are, and we need to know that before we can say where we are going. We can't otherwise recognize our destination if we don't know our destiny.[2]
MYRON MADDEN

I do not believe that we can put into anyone ideas which are not in him already. As a rule there are in everyone all sorts of good ideas, ready like tinder. But much of this tinder catches fire, or catches it successfully, only when it meets some flame or spark from outside, i.e. from some other person. Often, too, our own light goes out, and is rekindled by some experience we go through with a fellowman. Thus we have each of us cause to think with deep gratitude of those who have lighted the flames within us.[3]
ALBERT SCHWEITZER

Gracious God, I thank you for all of the people who through the years have encouraged me. May my gratitude be demonstrated through my own affirmation and support of others.

Help me to understand that the fleeting words I speak today may lodge forever within the memory of my child, my friend, my neighbor. May my voice be an instrument of your peace, a messenger of your grace. May I choose my words as if they were precious possessions to be given wisely and with care. For in truth, O Lord, I have no gift of greater value than the words I say this day: "Let the words of my mouth and the meditations of my heart be acceptable in Thy sight, O Lord, my strength and my redeemer." Amen.

EMBRACING THE ENEMY

ZECHARIAH IS AN UNUSUAL NAME FOR A Filipino. No doubt Zack Dayot's parents had heard of the name of the Old Testament prophet in church and had been captivated by its exotic ring. They broke family and cultural tradition and named their son Zechariah.

In Hebrew, Zechariah means "God remembers." This ancient Jewish prophet was born in the midst of military invasion and harsh captivity by the ruthless Babylonians. Zechariah grew into manhood to become a prophet and to preach a message whose central theme is that God is in control in troubled times. Though Zack Dayot's parents could not have foreseen the future, no more appropriate name could have been given to their son.

Zack grew up in the tranquil 1920s and 1930s. He married young and soon had children. It seemed that his life would be spent peacefully in the shadows of the world's stage, quietly sequestered away in the backwaters of the Philippine Islands.

Like his ancient namesake, Zack Dayot developed great religious sensitivity. He became a Christian and soon felt that he, too, was being called to be a prophet—to preach a word of love, hope, and responsibility to his people. Young Zack was just beginning his career as a minister when the storm clouds of World War II boiled up on the Pacific horizon and descended violently on the Philippines.

Within days of the bombing of the American fleet in Pearl Harbor, the Japanese army invaded the Philippines. As the

Japanese infantry crushed American and Filipino defense forces and forged their way inland, Zack watched in horror as his village, or *barrio*, came directly into the path of the advancing Japanese juggernaut.

A meeting of the barrio elders was called. The arrival of Japanese troops was imminent. It was decided that all of the men would flee into the jungle and hide. Certainly a barrio filled with women and children would be perceived as harmless and the Japanese would simply bypass them. If the men stayed, they might be mistaken as guerrilla forces and the barrio could be bombed or burned. The mayor agreed to remain and greet the Japanese, informing them of the barrio's defenseless position.

Unfortunately, the Japanese officers were enraged by the decision. The fact that the men were not present convinced the Japanese that, indeed, the men were guerrillas and were away from their village sniping at Japanese soldiers. A rash decision was made to use this barrio as an example for the rest of the province. Every house was burned, every animal slaughtered, and every woman and child shot. This would be a terrible warning to all Filipinos who resisted the Japanese army.

When Zack returned to his barrio, all that he had ever loved was destroyed. In a spasm of grief he buried his wife and small children and returned to the jungle to fight the Japanese. Shortly thereafter, he was captured in an ambush. He was beaten, tortured, and left in the night for dead. He awoke amidst a chilling monsoon rain and dragged himself into the shelter of the jungle.

Miraculously, Zack survived the war and faced the daunting task of starting all over again. Though young, he was no longer youthful. His innocence was gone. He had lost everything but his freedom and his belief in God.

Within a year or two Zack, remarried and a new child was born. He returned to his role as a Baptist minister. He also harbored a dream of going to seminary to complete his education.

Years sped by, children grew older, and Zack fulfilled his quest for education. Now Dr. Zechariah Dayot was a leading

122   figure in the Philippine Baptist Convention. The tragedy of World War II was fading away. He was happily married and fulfilled in his vocation.

Irony, however, rears its head in the most unexpected of times and places. During the year that Zack was president of the Philippine Baptist Convention, Baptist Christians in Japan decided that it was time to heal old wounds and publicly seek reconciliation with their Filipino brothers and sisters. The Japanese Baptist Convention voted to send a delegation of Japanese pastors to the Philippines and formally restore relationships with the estranged Filipino Baptists.

As president, Dr. Dayot was asked to go to the Manila airport and greet the Japanese pastors. Zack had thought that his wounds were healing, that his simmering anger and bitterness had abated. But when he pictured himself walking out on a runway and warmly greeting the Japanese, his heart turned cold. He could not join hands with the people who had killed his wife and children and left him for dead. He firmly refused to welcome the Japanese delegation.

Yet as the day approached when the Japanese pastors would arrive, Zack grew increasingly troubled. He was a man in turmoil, ripped by conflicting emotions and competing thoughts. He kept remembering that numbing and brutal moment of shoveling soil onto the graves of his children. He remembered his wife's ravaged body. But he also kept hearing the words of Jesus upon a Roman cross: "Father, forgive them for they know not what they do." Zack knew that forgiveness and undeserved grace is at the very heart of the gospel. Yet how can such blatant and intentional cruelty be forgiven?

There came a moment when a final decision had to be made and Zack made it. Catching a taxi, he rushed to the airport knowing that he had to do what he must do before he changed his mind. Standing on the tarmac with tears brimming his eyes, he the was the first to greet the Japanese pastors as they stepped on Philippine soil. As he bowed and then extended his hand in

fellowship, real healing began to take place in his life. Of course,
all that Zack felt at first was numbness interspersed by searing
raw emotion. But from that day forward, Zack was able to put
the past behind him. A handshake, a smile, a word of welcome
and reconciliation finally ended a war and set Zechariah Dayot
free. Now his prophetic words of love, grace, forgiveness, and
personal responsibility had a ring of authenticity as never before.
He became a symbol of Christian character for all Filipinos.

I first heard this story as a young boy. I can still picture old
Dr. Dayot walking across the campus of the Philippine Baptist
Seminary, thoughtfully mulling over his lecture notes, preparing to teach another generation of Filipino ministers. He always
had a gentle smile, and a humble bearing. I would stare at him
as if he were a great war hero, which he was. Time will never
erase his story from my memory.

But more than memory, the prophetic example of Zechariah
Dayot has continued to monitor and judge my actions. Just last
week I was visiting a former pastorate and saw a man who had
made my life difficult. For months I had seethed when I thought
of him. Now, I saw him standing at a distance.

I had the perfect opportunity to avoid him, to walk the other
way. No one would ever know the difference. I didn't need to talk
to him and I was sure he did not want to see me. But old Zack
grabbed me, gave me a nudge, and in a split second I decided to
call his name, to walk toward him, shake his hand, build a bridge
of friendship again. And it worked. The old memories have not
faded. But the animosity is now gone, the anger abated, and healing in my own heart is taking place.

It is a truism that we cannot heal and become whole until we
have embraced our enemy. The hatred, hostility, and venom
within us are like infection in a festering wound. The gaping
wound in our lives cannot be closed and scar tissue developed
until the infectious matter is removed. Most of us have to find
our own ways to embrace the enemy. Sometimes it is a handshake or a heart-to-heart conversation. Frequently it is a letter

quietly written, a hand upon a shoulder, a quiet word of encouragement or consolation. But there must be some overt and intentional reaching out to our enemy for forgiveness and healing to take place.

Life is too wonderful to be drained of vitality by the illness of unforgiveness. And too many people have wasted away and succumbed to slow deaths of bitterness. The example of Zechariah Dayot and of Jesus Christ point us to a much better way. We must embrace the enemy to be free from the pain of the past.

Forgiveness is the heart of the gospel, reconciliation its central theme. And pure and unmerited grace is the only hope that any of us have in this world or the next.

If you, O Lord, should mark iniquities,
Lord, who could stand?
But there is forgiveness with you,
so that you may be revered.
    PSALM 130:3-4

And forgive us our debts, as we have forgiven our debtors.
    MATTHEW 6:12

Then Peter came and said to him, "Lord, if another member of the church sins against me, how often should I forgive? As many as seven times? Jesus said to him, "Not seven times, but, I tell you, seventy-seven times.
    MATTHEW 18:21-22

Put away from you all bitterness and wrath and anger and wrangling and slander, together with all malice, and be kind to one another, tenderhearted, forgiving one another, as God in Christ has forgiven you.
    EPHESIANS 4:31-32

To be a Christian means to forgive the inexcusable,
because God has forgiven the inexcusable in you.[1]
C. S. LEWIS

*Forgiveness is the fragrance the violet sheds on the heel that
has crushed it.*[2]
MARK TWAIN

*One day General James Oglethorpe said to John Wesley, "I
never forgive." Wesley retorted, "Then I hope, sir, that you
never sin."*[3]
JOHN WESLEY

The glory of Christianity is to conquer by forgiveness.[4]
WILLIAM BLAKE

Dear God, I have not been subjected to the ravages of war, the loss of all family, the murder of friends, the destruction of my country. Yet hate and malice can be far more subtle. And I have done my fair share of loathing.

I confess that there are people who have hurt me and I have been slow to pardon. Their petty words ring in my ears; their injurious actions play over and over in my memory. I touch the edge of the razor each day and remember the sharp, swift sting of injury. There is an evil comfort in coddling a malicious memory.

Yet, Lord, I want to forgive. For the idle razor when touched still cuts. And I have been bled of the vitality of your spirit.

Allow me to let go, to embrace my enemy. May I remember that my Lord is not asking me to do what he has not done. Father, help me to forgive. Amen.

RESTORATION

I FIRST SAW THE PAINTING IN THE recessed shadows of a musty antique shop hanging modestly on the back wall. The frame caught my eye, the carved and gilded molding announcing nineteenth-century workmanship. Threading my way through a maze of stacked and dusty furniture, I stood before the painting and peered through the dimness to glimpse its subject. The canvas had turned dark with age, the colors drab and muted, with images hidden by layers of dirt, smoke, and grime. I could detect the outline of a few trees, the fading pattern of a skyline. It was, or had been, a landscape.

"How much do you want for this painting?" I asked the portly antique dealer as he sauntered over.

"Well, it's not much of a painting, is it?" he said, clinching a brier pipe between yellowed teeth. "I bought if for the frame. It's a nice frame. And I've priced it for the frame alone. I'll take a hundred dollars."

Turning back to the painting, an antique collector's instinct tugged at me. "If this painting is worth anything at all then that's a bargain," I thought. "But it would be risky to buy it. I don't need the frame. And I don't know if the painting will clean up, or how much it will cost to have it professionally restored, or even if I'll like it if it does clean up well."

"What do you know about the painting?" I asked the dealer.

"Bought it several years ago at an estate sale somewhere in Georgia. It was in a farm house. The painting hung over a fire place. That's why it's so dark. Years of soot and smoke messed it up. It's signed in the bottom right corner."

I stared at the painting for a long time. An original nineteenth-century oil painting for a hundred dollars is a steal. But what was under the smudge and grit?

Carrying the painting outside, I studied it in the sunlight. I could now detect a narrow stream coursing across the center of the canvas, a slim English punt gliding on it's surface. There was the vague image of a man sitting in the stern fishing with a cane pole. My curiosity was snared. On rash impulse I bought the painting and fought back pangs of guilt.

I have a friend who restores paintings. After driving to his studio, I sheepishly introduced him to my tarnished gamble. He placed the painting under ultraviolet light, his trained eyes detecting what I could not see.

"Well, I don't think you've found a Rembrandt or Goya," he quipped. "But its a nice composition. Definitely English. Artist probably a student."

"The canvas is brittle. It'll need to be relined and restretched. The old lacquer finish will have to be removed. But the major problem is smoke damage. A mild ammonia emulsion will probably clean her up. What you'll have when I'm finished is anybody's guess. Won't be a masterpiece, but it could be a fine painting."

Knowing that I did not want to hear the answer, I popped the big question, "How much will it cost to do all of that?"

"If I'm going to do it, I want to do it right," he sparked with professional pride. "Unless I run into something unexpected, it'll cost around two hundred dollars."

I swallowed hard. The stakes were getting high, but I was beyond the point of no return. My only hope of coming out of this deal was to get the canvas cleaned. A beautiful nineteenth-century oil painting at three hundred dollars is still a bargain. But only if I liked the painting.

"Clean her up," I said with all of the confidence of a tight rope walker in a hail storm. "We'll give this old fellow another chance."

Two weeks later I picked up the painting. I was not only relieved; I was pleased. Though the mood was still dusky, a beautiful landscape at sunset could now be seen. The colors of the sky—violet, vermillion, amber—were subdued, yet beautiful. The man in the punt wore a straw boater hat, white shirt, and vest—clearly Victorian. In the background was a stucco English cottage with a thatched roof which could not be seen prior to the cleaning. It was a beautiful pastoral scene, and I was proud to own the painting.

Even though I winced as I wrote the check for the restoration, I felt good as I drove home. A work of art had been saved from ruin. Now a special moment captured a century ago still lived and an artist's heart still beat. At least, this was the passionate logic I presented to my wife, Beth, when she balanced our checkbook. I'm not sure she agreed. But she didn't brain me.

For the last five years the painting has hung in our living room (not over the mantle piece!). Many times I have stared at the canvas, wondering who the man in the boat was, where the stream is located, how an English painting ever came to be hung in a Georgia farm house. Gradually the painting and I have become friends. But more than this, the old painting has slowly come to symbolize something of personal and spiritual insight to me.

I, too, am getting older whether I want to or not. And, like the painting, I seem to be growing "dimmer" with age. The soot and grit—the residue of burning up the years—has covered me and I often feel that I am not the same bright and vibrant person that I was years ago.

The light of idealism and virtue has slowly grown dimmer. I have seen too much! Many adolescent visions of goodness have been shattered and naive dreams have faded in the night of experience. If I have become wiser, wisdom has not always brought happiness or hope. And the weight of mistakes, moral dilemmas, and outright sin—mine and others—have grown heavy and oppressive.

If I am lucky, I have lived half of my life, long enough to know my frailty in all its crafty and subtle manifestations. Long enough to know that try as I might, I will probably not fundamentally change or reshape my personality. The good and the bad were grafted together long ago; my trunk is now solid and fused. I am who I am.

Many of us, if we are honest, assess our adult selves and know that, even if we have been successful, there is much that we do not like about ourselves. Adulthood has changed us. We sometimes marvel that others seem to genuinely like us, even love and admire us. Do they see through the smoke better than we do?

Using the unique human ability of self-transcendence, we watch in horror as we grow irritable and snap at our children, saying things we never thought we'd say.

When one of my bright eyed and exuberant sons comes bursting into my study and shouts his fondest invitation, "Dad, would you come outside and throw the football with me?" I hesitate, look at unfinished work, and fumble for an excuse not to do the very thing that I used to love to do. The beautiful, frolicking child within me is struggling for life, gasping for breath, dying in an adult world. Joy and playfulness have been covered up.

And our spouses? Do we ever act like we are in love anymore? Has the soot grown so thick, the lacquer so opaque, that we cannot see their beauty? I look at my wife and say to myself, "If I cannot love, feel passion, and treat affectionately this most beautiful and gentlest of women, then my heart has turned to stone." And yet, many couples live their lives together grown far too comfortable with the numbness of dull routine. We take each other for granted. Romance, the heartbeat of life, is stilled by time and neglect.

In the midst of my adulthood darkness, I am haunted by the awareness that I am not what God created me to be. I barely reflect the image he painted on the canvas of my life. Perhaps this is why in his midlife years Jesus said that we cannot experience the kingdom of God unless we are born again, unless we

130   become like children and recapture the vision, the color, and the vibrancy of life.

Maybe all of this sounds abstract or mushy. Perhaps you think I'm morbid, in some kind of crisis and down on myself. I'm not. Or maybe you know exactly what I'm talking about and have experienced it in your own life. But the real question I'm asking is: "How, like the old painting, can we be restored? How can color, brilliance, beauty, and perspective be brought back through the soot and smoke of the years?" This is a pressing issue for all who have lived long enough and deep enough. I believe that an answer can be found in the life of the apostle Paul.

How did it happen that the apostle Paul stumbled onto a concept he called "grace" and made it the heart of his thought and theology? Why did Paul seize onto this word "grace" like a drowning man grasping a life preserver? I suspect I know why.

At midlife, Paul was successful, responsible, devoutly religious, and very adult. But Paul was unhappy to the core of his heart. He was tired of himself; he didn't like the pompous, striving adult that had smothered the child within him. He was frightened by how entrapped he was by "a thorn in the flesh" that he desperately sought to overcome. Yet he was impaled by whatever compulsive power the thorn held. Paul was too smart not to see the smoke and soot for what it was. He knew that he was a "Hebrew of the Hebrews" and yet a fraud. He knew the canvas of his life was darkening.

Something finally broke. Paul called it an encounter with the risen Lord. You may call it a vision, a revelation, a miracle, a nervous break down or whatever. But something broke. And it was more than Paul's heart.

Paul literally got knocked off his high horse while traveling on the road to Damascus when a bright light struck like lightning and shone through his darkness. He was blinded. And when his vision was restored, the world looked different. His picture of himself had altered. The old canvas had been restored.

What happened? Paul simply said that he had been "saved by grace." What did he mean?

Whatever characterized the light that shone down upon Paul, I am confident that there was certainly more than just brilliance and brightness. There was also *warmth*, a radiating warmth that embraced and enveloped him. It was a warmth that in a suprarational way communicated to Paul that he was loved just as he was, that he did not need to change, or be better, or do more, or sin less in order to be loved by the Source of this great light. It was like being picked up and cuddled by an affectionate father or being drawn to a mother's breast. And though the entire experience was frightening, the one feeling that Paul could never shake was that in this brief encounter he felt like a child again. A child who was accepted and loved not because of what he had done or had not done but only because he was a child. God's child.

Paul Tillich is one of the greatest theologians of the twentieth century. In a sermon preached in 1948, he spoke of grace in a most powerful way:

> Grace strikes us when we are in great pain and restlessness. It strikes us when we walk through the dark valley of a meaningless and empty life. It strikes us when we feel that our separation is deeper than usual, because we have violated another life, a life which we loved, or from which we were estranged. It strikes us when our disgust for our own being, our indifference, our weakness, our hostility, and our lack of direction and composure have become intolerable to us. It strikes us when, year after year, the longed-for perfection of life does not appear, when the old compulsions reign within us as they have for decades, when despair destroys all joy and courage. Sometimes at that moment a wave of light breaks into our darkness, and it is as though a voice were saying: "You are accepted. *You are accepted*, accepted by that

which is greater than you, and the name of which you do not know. Do not ask for the name now; perhaps you will find it later. Do not try to do anything now; perhaps later you will do much. Do not seek for anything; do not perform anything; do not intend anything. *Simply accept the fact that you are accepted!*"[1]

Years ago I first read these words as a twenty-four year old, newly married seminary student. Even then I sensed that Tillich's words pointed to truth. But it was a truth I was aware that I had not yet experienced. And so I wrote the words on a note card and saved them for another day. Now, twenty years later, my canvas is darker, my experience deeper, and the light of truth shines through. Tillich's words are now my words. Maybe your words as well.

However, though Tillich is absolutely correct, accepting grace is easier said than done. I have personally found that the hardest thing in life is to accept myself and to accept self-forgiveness. And at the root of most of the problems that I deal with as a pastor and counselor are people's inability to love, forgive, and accept themselves.

Yet, if we do not accept the grace of God and continually condemn and criticize ourselves, we are like a drowning man fighting against a riptide. If you are caught in a powerful riptide, the worst thing that you can do is fight against its powerful pull. But as the tide drags you away from shore and safety, the most powerful instincts within you scream, "Swim like crazy! Beat this thing! Use all your strength to overcome the ocean or you will die!"

But experienced swimmers know that the only way to survive in a riptide is to relax and float, to lie on your back and let the current carry you along until the tide plays out and then you can swim to shore.

So it is in the riptide of sin, despair, and self-condemnation. Sometimes fighting against our own faults and weakness makes perfect sense. And so you strive to do better, pray harder, have more determination and self-discipline. But the harder you try, and the more you fight against yourself, the further that you are pulled down. Gradually you drown in the despair of your own lack of self-forgiveness and egotistical pride.

Grace is the permission to float in the buoyancy of God's love. Grace is the realization that "being better and doing better" does not increase God's love for you. And when you really understand this and begin to relax and float, the rip tide that has bound you slowly loses its power. Soon, by the grace of God, you begin to float free.

Grace and forgiveness are at the heart of the good news of Christianity. They are the simplest and yet most difficult of truths to understand. Usually we cannot experience the power of grace and really believe we are accepted much before our middle-age years. We have to live a long time first. The canvas of life must grow dark and dim. Only then can light break through. Only then are we ready to be restored and reborn again and again and again.

> *Have mercy on me, O God,*
> *according to your steadfast love;*
> *according to your abundant mercy*
> *blot out my transgressions.*
> *Wash me thoroughly from my iniquity,*
> *and cleanse me from my sin.*
> *For I know my transgressions,*
> *and my sin is ever before me. . . .*
> *Create in me a clean heart, O God,*
> *and put a new and right spirit within me.*
> PSALM 51:1-3, 10

Do not be conformed to this world, but be transformed by the renewing of your minds, so that you may discern what is the will of God—what is good and acceptable and perfect.
ROMANS 12:2

For we do not have a high priest who is unable to sympathize with our weaknesses, but we have one who in every respect has been tested as we are, yet without sin. Let us therefore approach the throne of grace with boldness, so that we may receive mercy and find grace to help in time of need.
HEBREWS 4:15-16

Man is born broken; he lives by mending. The grace of God is the glue.[2]
EUGENE O'NEILL

Every story of conversion is the story of a blessed defeat.[3]
C. S. LEWIS

Gracious God, we cannot alter or slow the aging process. And as we grow older, the picture of our lives grows dim. Much is hidden in shadow. The flames of life have coated us with soot and stain. Restore us to beauty and clarity of vision.

Help us to see that you, O Master, love old paintings. You love the patina of our years, the layered texture of our lives, the history that is ours, and the stories that we tell.

May we know now that your grace is sufficient for our restoration. We trust ourselves to your mercy and grace. Amen.

GLIMPSES OF
TIME AND
ETERNITY

THE COBBLER'S NAIL

17

I WAS RUSHING TO A MEETING IN DOWN-town Charleston, South Carolina. Glancing at my watch, I had two minutes before I would be late and I could not find a parking space. Already I had circled the block three times. Frantically, I drove in ever widening circles looking for any place—legal or illegal—to park. Finally, six blocks from my meeting, I found an empty space securely guarded by a parking meter.

I jumped out of the car and fumbled for coins to feed the meter. Striding, nearly loping, down the sidewalk, I soon rediscovered how hot and humid August days are in Charleston. Throwing my sports coat over my shoulder and loosening my tie, I charged on.

I had not gone more than two blocks when I crossed a street, bounded up on the side walk, tripped, and fell flat on my face. The heel of my shoe had caught in a metal grate, pitching me forward and ripping the loafer off my foot. Hopping up, I put first things first, frantically looking to see who had seen me make a fool of myself. To my vast relief, I was alone. Only then did I dare grimace in pain.

When I reached down to pick up my loafer, I discovered that the heel had been completely sheered off and that cobbler nails were sticking through the sole. I obviously could not wear the shoe or walk the remaining six blocks in my socks. Exploding, I began to say things I do not want to repeat. It was obvious I would not make my meeting.

Gazing around as if seeing my surroundings for the first time, I noticed that I was in an older part of town. Little had changed on this block since World War II. The weathered store fronts covered by faded canvas awnings spoke of another era, my parents' generation. Some of the sun-bleached advertisements pictured my childhood in the early 1950s. Many of the shops had been closed, boarded up with large sheets of plywood. A mom-and-pop grocery store still struggled to stay in business. And a used book shop opened its door to a dark and musty world within. The block looked like a time warp waiting for restoration.

As I turned to peer through the plate glass window of the store in front of me, my mouth flew open. Of all things, I had tripped and sprawled right in front of a shoe repair store. Grinning and holding my shoe in hand, I walked into the repair shop in my stocking feet. I might make my meeting yet.

The cobbler was a large black man, bullet headed and balding, with a long white apron shielding his broad girth. Wire-rimmed glasses perched on the tip of his wide nose. He was standing behind a counter, lost in his work, gluing a half-sole on a worn shoe. There was a feeling as if this man had been in the store forever, generation upon generation.

Walking toward the counter, I was overcome with the pleasant smell of the place. The richness of the aroma of leather was mixed with distinct whiffs of shoe polish, boot black, and glue. There was an earthiness about it all, a scent of old world craftsmanship.

The cobbler flashed me a big grin, "Bout busted yourself, didn't you? I saw all that. Good thing you're young. You hurt?"

"Nope. Just my pride," I retorted. "But my shoe's about had it. My heel clipped that sidewalk grate and ripped clear off. Do you think you could repair this in a hurry? I'm late for a meeting."

"I can fix it. But I'm up to my elbows in this glue. Can't stop a glue job half through. Have a seat and I'll get to you as fast as I can. And relax, Man. That hurrying is gonna kill you. Nearly did."

Turning, I saw an antique Coke machine in a corner. I bought a Coke, a pack of peanut-butter cheese crackers, and slumped down in a chair against a wall. Only then did I realize how tired and thirsty I was.

As I fumbled to open the crackers, I remembered the first time I tasted their peanut-butter saltiness. I was eleven years old and was spending the afternoon with my grandmother. She pulled a pack of cheese crackers from her bulging purse and gave them to me along with a ten cent bottle of Coke. An addiction was born that day. There has never been anything else that has tasted better for this Georgia boy.

As I grinned with the memory, the coiled spring within me began to unwind and I breathed easier. My heart stopped pounding. The meeting didn't matter any more. I had missed it and that was that. As I wiggled my toes inside my socks, I began to feel like a kid going barefoot on the first day of spring.

Overhead an ancient ceiling fan slowly turned, humming and moving a breeze across my face. I leaned my head back against the wall, kicked my feet up on a box, and closed my eyes. "What would it have been like to live in a day before cars, telephones, electricity, and appointment books?" I wondered. "What would it be like to go to sleep and sit here all afternoon?" It'd feel pretty doggone good, I decided.

As if in a dream, I watched the cobbler move slowly and deliberately repairing his shoes. A radio was playing softly in the background and he was humming along with the black gospel choir. Occasionally he would break out in song, a resonant bass voice rising up out of the depths of living. I didn't know this man, only his name, *Willie Johnson*, painted on the plate glass window. But I liked him.

Time passed quickly. Thirty minutes elapsed and I was feeling a peace like you're supposed to get in church but I seldom do. It was a peace that comes with silence, with sitting still and getting in touch with feelings and thoughts, with allowing the muscles in your face to relax and your anger to pass away.

140   Sitting there listening to the hum of the fan, I recalled the
words to a verse I had learned as a child and had seldom thought
of since.

> For want of a nail, a shoe was lost,
> For want of a shoe, a horse was lost,
> For want of a horse, a battle was lost,
> For want of a battle, a kingdom was lost,
> And all for the want of a horseshoe nail.

Most of us lose a significant part of our lives in the blur of busy-
ness and haste. We are much too pushed and frantic to hear a fan
hum, to really taste a Coke, to notice the ambiance of a neigh-
borhood as we drive madly by. It takes the loss of a heel and the
need of a nail to slow us down and make us savor life again.

Quite often the loss of a heel becomes a heart attack, a nag-
ging cold, an ulcer or colitis. The loss of a heel can be a divorce,
a resignation, a bankruptcy, or a professional disappointment.
Many things can trip us up and pitch us on our face. And most
of these experiences are painful. All of these things tell us that we
had better pick ourselves up and slow down.

I often work too long and too hard to enjoy my children.
They'll be grown before I know it. What a tragedy it will be if I
am a far better grandfather than a father.

I am frequently too busy as the minister of a large church to be
sensitive to the needs of my people. Meetings, agendas, and goals
get in the way of listening to people's hearts, of seeing the glint in
their eyes, of enjoying the beauty of their smiles and the delight
of their stories.

As a husband, how in the world can I sleep with the same
woman every night, cradle her in my arms, smell the fragrance of
her hair, feel her warm breath against my shoulder, and still go
for days without a conversation of real meaning or a new insight
into the depth of her soul?

It happens to us all. And it comes from living on the fast
track, surviving in a modern world. In rushing to save time, we

lose time. And in living lives of oppressive work, we sacrifice the 141
very things for which we labor.

Sitting in that shoe shop, I became glad that I had lost the
heel of my shoe. It gave me a chance to find a cobbler's nail. And
if I can remember that glimpse of wisdom, that window in time,
perhaps the kingdom will not be lost.

The Lord is my shepherd;
I shall not want.
He maketh me to lie down in green pastures:
He leadeth me beside the still waters.
He restoreth my soul.
    PSALM 23:1-3 (KJV)

He gives power to the faint,
and strengthens the powerless.
Even youths will faint and be weary,
and the young will fall exhausted;
but those who wait for the Lord
shall renew their strength;
they shall mount up with wings like eagles,
they shall run and not be weary,
they shall walk and not faint.
    ISAIAH 40:29-31

He said to them [the disciples], "Come away to a deserted
place all by yourselves and rest a while." For many were
coming and going, and they had no leisure even to eat.
    MARK 6:31

Without even knowing it, we are assaulted by a high note
of urgency all the time. We end up pacing ourselves to the
city rhythm whether or not it's our own. In time we even

grow hard of hearing to the rest of the world. Like a violin-
ist stuck next to the timpani, we may lose the ability to
hear our own instrument.[1]
ELLEN GOODMAN

One day [the apostle John] was found playing with a tame
partridge. A narrower and more rigid brother rebuked him
for thus wasting his time, and John answered: "The bow
that is always bent will soon cease to shoot straight."[2]
WILLIAM BARCLAY

What is this life if, full of care,
We have not time to stand and stare?[3]
W. H. DAVIES

The future is something which everyone reaches at the rate
of sixty minutes an hour, whatever he does, whoever he is.[4]
C. S. LEWIS

Dear Lord, all my life I have been in a hurry. Now, I wonder why?
When I recall my fondest memories, most were spent in rest and
leisure. It is the busy moments that are forgotten, blurred by the
frantic rush of time.

Yet, it is hard to slow me down, Lord. I fear the silence. I grow
uneasy with my thoughts. I resist the sound of my beating heart.
Hectic lives are a marvelous narcotic for sane and sober Puritans.

Father, slow me down before the wear and tear of years
cripples me. Give me your permission to rest and play and
enjoy. Lead me to green pastures and still water. And restore my
soul. Amen.

"WHEN I HAVE FEARS . . ."

18

JOHN WAS A YOUNG MAN WHOSE LIFE had not been easy. His father was killed in an accident when he was eight. His mother, whom he adored, had died of a prolonged disease when he was thirteen. Heart broken, the boy lost himself in books and the quiet solace they can bring.

A handsome fellow, John was slight in stature yet plucky and passionate. His intensity got him into many childhood fights. He won most of them. Life itself, however, was the biggest battle that lay before him, and he threw himself into the fray with vigor.

Having nursed his mother in her illness, John decided to go to medical school. Working his way through the difficult regimen of study, he often turned to poetry and writing as a way of escape and expression. Midway through medical school he began to a achieve modest literary success which pitched him into a vocational quandary. Would he play it safe and be a doctor or cast away caution and security to become a writer? Against everyone's advise, John dropped out of medical school when he was close to graduation and determined to be a poet.

Very quickly he became immersed in the literary world. A few of his poems were published and achieved critical acclaim. But a rising star is also a rising target and many critics began to review John's work harshly. Their jealous words stung him and pricked his fledgling insecurity. He feared for future success.

Struggling through the pathos of his early twenties, the young poet fell head over heels in love. At the same time, his

144   youngest brother, whom he deeply loved, contracted the same
lung disease from which his mother had died. Returning home
to nurse and support his brother, he remained with him until his
death several months later.

Burying his brother, John contemplated marriage and his
future. Though in love, his courtship had often been stormy. He
was not sure he would make it to the alter, though he could not
deny he was in love. But more than love, the issue of mortality
hounded him. Burying his brother had ripped the last vestiges of
innocence away. With good reason he feared that the same con-
genital predisposition for lung disease that had killed his mother
and brother would soon claim him as well. Hounded by a poet's
sensitivity, he reeled in a world of worry, anxiety, and depression.

One summer's night after a lengthy walk on a beach, the
young man composed a sonnet penned with the ink of his own
life's blood:

> When I have fears that I may cease to be
>   Before my pen has glean'd my teeming brain,
> Before high-piled books in charact'ry
>   Hold like rich garners the full ripen'd grain;
> When I behold upon the night's starr'd face
>   Huge cloudy symbols of a high romance,
> And think that I may never live to trace
>   Their shadows with the magic hand of chance;
> And when I feel, fair creature of an hour,
>   That I shall never look upon thee more,
> Never have relish in the faery power
>   Of unreflecting love;—then on the shore
> Of the wide world I stand alone, and think
>   Till love and fame to nothingness do sink.[1]

This sonnet touches the pulse of all who have ever loved and
yearned, who have ever wanted to give expression to truth
through art, who have ever wanted to leave their small, unique

fingerprint upon the window of life. We all have fears that we will die much too soon before our life's work is done and our vast loves and dreams are fulfilled.

Tragically, this young man's fears were founded. Three years later he died of "the family disease," tuberculosis, having never achieved literary fame or known the joys of marriage and family.

In the final months of his life he penned these words to his sweetheart, "'If I should die,' said I to myself, 'I have left no immortal work behind me—nothing to make my friends proud of my memory—but I have lov'd the principle of beauty in all things, and if I had time I would have made myself remember'd.'"

The young man who went to his unmarked grave in 1821 at the age of twenty-five was John Keats, known today as perhaps the greatest of the English Romantic poets. Though over half of his work was not published until after his death, his genius could not be suppressed. Because he had "lov'd the principle of beauty in all things" and took the risk to pursue it boldly during his brief years of life, his words and spirit still move the hearts of many decades later.

I had not "met" John Keats until five years ago. By chance I received a volume of his poetry through a classics book club. I would have never bought the book had it been in a book store. But because it was sent to me, I thumbed through its pages. Immediately the biographical sketch of Keats riveted me. It spoke of real life, filled with passion, pathos and fire. And his poetry pealed forth truth. John Keats has become a lifelong friend.

In Keats I have met a man who was honest enough to say that he feared death. Not so much that he feared the pain of death—we all do—but because he feared that he would die before "my pen has glean'd my teeming brain, before high-piled books in charact'ry hold like rich garners the full ripen'd grain." Being a writer, I identify with this. There are a lot more books I've outlined in my head. And I'm going to be disappointed if I never write them.

146   How about you? Many who read these words couldn't care
less if they ever write a book or publish a poem. That's not your
gift or passion. But there is probably a dream within you that you
want to accomplish, a goal you'd like to reach, a relationship
you'd like to share, a journey you'd like to complete. Yet death
can rob us all of that which we wish to accomplish.

As I have reflected on the life of John Keats, I have come to
see that what is really important is not what death takes from us
but what we contribute to life.

Keats was a man who took chances, who risked his life to
be a poet. He was a man who deeply loved and cherished his
sweetheart, Fanny Brawne, until the end. And most of all, he
continued to write with passion, even when all hope of literary
success dimmed away. Because he "lov'd the principle of beauty
in all things" he could not refuse to express that beauty as long as
his mortal lungs had breath.

Keats has caused me not so much to fear death as to value
life, not so much to fear the end but to relish and respect each
day that is mine to live. I cannot control the number of my days,
but I can decide how each day will be lived.

I think of Jesus Christ, my ultimate example for living. He
lived only thirty-three years, and thirty of those as an unknown
carpenter. He never wrote a book. All of his brilliant parables
survived second hand, penned by someone else. And yet his
life changed human history and eternal destiny as no other
life. He, too, lived with ultimate purpose. He, too, went to his
grave a defeated young man. Yet, he above all others, received
immortality.

The issue is not how long we live but how we live. And the
issue is not our ability but God's ability. A life that is directed
toward the expression of love and truth is a life that transcends
death. It is a life that keeps living in a poem or a painting, a student or a grandchild, in the memories of those we have loved
and cared for. John Claypool has written:

For some time now, the conviction has been growing on me that finally there are only two realities—love and fear. Love is confidence that there is enough, and therefore one can live with courage and generosity in the assurance that whatever one faces, being sons and daughters of abundance, we can make the best of things. On the other hand, fear is the suspicion there is not enough and never will be. This leads to a life-style of anxiety and a kind of siege-mentality. Obviously, these polar opposites have the power to cancel out each other. "Love casts out fear," according to the Epistle of I John, and fear casts out love, according to our own experience. I am never less fearful than when I am most loving, and never less loving than when I am most fearful. Each of us has a choice—in which of these primal realities will we plant our lives?[2]

On those nights when I look into the vault of darkest heaven and "have fears that I may cease to be," I spend some time with John Keats. I reflect on the life of Jesus. And I decide again to get on with my life, to make each day rich, productive, and enjoyable.

The future is in God's hands. Today is in my hands. This book needs to be completed. My family needs to be loved. My church needs to be shepherded. And so much more. And so much more.

I am so thankful for the gift of life! For this day!

But strive first for the kingdom of God and his righteousness, and all these things will be given to you as well. So do not worry about tomorrow, for tomorrow will bring worries of its own. Today's trouble is enough for today.
MATTHEW 6:33-34

Not that I have already obtained this or have already reached the goal; but I press on to make it my own, because Christ Jesus has made me his own. Beloved, I do no consider that I have made it my own; but this one thing I do: forgetting what lies behind and straining forward to what lies ahead, I press on toward the goal for the prize of the heavenly call of God in Christ Jesus.
    PHILIPPIANS 3:12-16

So let us not grow weary in doing what is right, for we will reap at harvest-time, if we do not give up. So then, whenever we have an opportunity, let us work for the good of all, and especially for those of the family of faith.
    GALATIANS 6:9-10

Nothing is worth more than this day.[3]
    JOHANN WOLFGANG VON GOETHE

God give me work
Till my life shall end
And life
Till my work is done[4]
    WINFRED HOLTBY

There are persons who shape their lives by the fear of death, and persons who shape their lives by the joy and satisfaction of life. The former live dying; the latter die living. I know that fate may stop me tomorrow, but death is an irrelevant contingency. Whenever it comes, I intend to die living.[5]
    HORACE KALLEN

In the spring of 1970, within six shocking weeks, my good friend's teenage daughter died of an embolism, my husband's best friend died of cancer at age thirty-nine, and my mother's heart failed just short of her sixty-third birthday. I lost my fear of flying that spring—I'll fly on anything now—for I had become re-acquainted with mortality and I recognized that even if I stayed grounded all of my life, I would still die.[6]

JUDITH VIORST

Dear God, I must admit that sometimes I feel afraid. I stand by too many death beds and gaze into too many graves to pretend that death does not exist. I cannot suppress it's chilling presence from my life. Yet, O Lord, I would be a fool to allow the fear of death to steal the pleasure of my life.

I am pricked by the memory of a friend, dying of cancer. He looked at me with his bright eyes and said, "I feared I would be the dead walking among the living. But I have discovered that I am the living walking among the dead."

O God, may I hear his words of caution and of promise. May I be one who is fully alive, fully joyous, fully aware and grateful for each day that is mine. May I live my life to the fullest, never satisfied that my love and work are done. Amen.

19 SYMBOLS

IN A WAY, DEATH IS NO STRANGER TO ME. I've lost my father, my grandparents, some uncles and aunts, and other close friends of our family. As a pastor for twenty years, I have stood by numerous deathbeds and looked into the depths of many graves. Along with doctors and morticians, I should be steeled against the trauma of death. For a while I thought I was. But I'm not. Not at all.

Several months ago when I was at a convention in west Texas, the phone rang in my hotel room. Answering, I heard a high school friend, Guy Pearson, say, "Scott, if I'm tracking you down in Amarillo, you probably know it's bad news. And, it is. Joe Cleveland died today. Had a heart attack. He was dead before they got him to the hospital. I knew you'd want to know. I'm really sorry."

Stunned, I hung up the phone and sat down on the bed. Tears would not come. Only dumb disbelief and a dim awareness of mounting terror. I got up, pulled on a jacket, and walked around the hotel parking lot. I wanted to run, to escape. Even the big, blue, west Texas sky could not brighten the darkness that overwhelmed me. "My God! I just can't believe Joe Cleveland is dead!" I mumbled over and over. It's all I could think. All I could say.

Joe and I had been close friends in high school in Fort Valley, Georgia. We had played football together and had helped each other survive algebra and Latin. Our high school sweethearts were best friends, and we were a natural foursome.

We were both late-bloomers. I was tall and skinny, and Joe was short and pugnacious. "Little Joe" we called him, partly because he wanted to grow more than anything and partly because he looked a lot like Michael Landon on the television series *Bonanza*. He was winsome and handsome, and he'd fight a bear with a stick.

Following high school graduation, Joe enrolled at Clemson University and announced that he was going to play football. All of his buddies smirked behind straight faces and thought, "Sure you are, Cleveland. Sure you are. Wait until you're a blocking dummy for a few weeks and we'll see about that."

We all grinned, that is, until we heard the news that he had not only made the team but was actually playing in games. Then Little Joe wasn't Little Joe anymore. Just to spite us, I think, he grew to stand six foot two and weigh two hundred pounds. He made a great defensive back, and all his small town friends were proud, even his envious buddies.

While walking around the hotel parking lot, I thought about these things. But for some reason what I remembered most was a nameless winter day when we were both sixteen and were running together to get in shape for spring football practice. Dressed in gray sweats, we were striding down a red clay road winding through a peach orchard. The sun was setting and the sky was on fire, the leafless peach trees stark and silhouetted. I remember looking over at Joe and he was sweating and smiling. Breathing hard, he was in his competitive element, grinning because we were secretly racing each other back to the gym. The setting sun, the smiling face, the silhouetted peach trees will be in my mind forever.

I didn't make Joe's funeral—partly because I could not leave the conference and partly because Georgia is a thousand miles away. But mostly because I was scared. Scared stiff because this was the first peer friend I have ever lost to death. Scared because Joe died one day after his forty-third birthday leaving a beautiful wife and twelve-year-old twins. Scared because Joe's death screams out the warning that life is not fair but is filled with tragedy and can literally be one hell of an experience.

No, for me, it was safer to stay in Texas. But not even Texas and an Alamo mentality could protect me from the shattering news that I, too, am old enough to die. I can no longer leap over buildings and stop bullets. Middle age now tells me that my lease on immortality is over. Joe beat me to the grave.

Not long after Joe's death, I traveled back to Macon, Georgia, for a trustees meeting at my alma mater, Mercer University. I knew it was time to visit Joe's widow, Debbie. Though I greatly looked forward to seeing her and the children, I didn't know what I would say. I was sure that "preacher talk" wouldn't work. It seldom does. And a hug can only last so long.

Over the years I have learned that words can never convey the greatest truths and mysteries of life. And when words will not work, we must always turn to symbols. Somehow symbols get past our rational left brain and lodge themselves deeply into the primal depths of our intuitive right brain. Symbols do not get mired down in the limited morass of human reason. They root right down into the marrow of life.

Before I left Texas, my wife, Beth, and I talked about what we could do to symbolically express to Debbie, her son, Blake, and her daughter, Nita, our deepest feelings. But more than our feelings of grief, we wanted to express our common faith in the ultimate goodness of life and the loving care of God. We decided to buy three silver crosses to be worn as necklaces. With three small jewelry boxes in my coat pocket, I set off for Georgia.

When I called to ask Debbie out to dinner, she wouldn't hear of it. Instead she invited me over and cooked a wonderful meal. Joe's dad, "Pop," was there and Blake and Nita curtailed their busy schedules to sit around the table and talk. When

twelve year olds will stay home and visit with "Dad's friend," it
is a rare honor.

After dinner, Debbie, the kids, and I went into the den and sat around a crackling fire. In two weeks it would be Christmas and Debbie had decorated a beautiful Christmas tree. I marveled at her fortitude and courage. Decorating the tree must have been a lonely and painful experience. But she had gritted her teeth and done what needed to be done for the children.

There is a certain silence that only comes with expectancy. Seated around the fireplace I sensed a hush amidst the crackling of the flames that said to me, "Whatever you've got to say, say it now." I looked at Joe's daughter, Nita, saw her father's eyes, and reached in my pocket for the crosses.

"I brought you something from Texas," I began, far more timid and flustered than I sounded. "Beth and I want you to have these gifts from us, and in a moment I'll tell you why."

I handed Debbie, Blake, and Nita each a small, wrapped package. Blake, with no courtly pretense, ripped into his first. As he held his cross necklace in his rough, boyish hand, I started to say apologetically, "Blake, I know you think this is a weird present. . . ," but Blake cut me off with his own expression of, "Gosh, Dr. Walker, I always wanted one of these." I was surprised and relieved.

Soon I heard myself saying, "Beth and I want to give you these crosses for a reason. We thought a long time about finding you something that might help you through this painful moment in your lives. These crosses came to mind."

"A cross is a symbol. And a symbol is something that expresses a truth we can't quite put into words," I stammered, realizing that my talk of symbols was pressing the patience and comprehension of twelve year olds. Yet they were listening intently.

"Blake, your cross symbolizes that God has felt every pain that you and I will ever know. When Jesus was crucified and died a horrible death, God experienced the same pain and sorrow that you are feeling now with the loss of your dad. Sometimes we feel that we are all alone in our sorrow, that nobody else understands. I want this cross to remind you that God loves you very much and understands everything that you are feeling. You can tell God about every thought and every emotion you experience and God will understand. God is a God who feels with you."

Blake shook his head, wrapping the silver chain around his knuckles, and looking intently at the cross. Gazing at Nita, I took a deep breath, tears brimming my eyes, and reached for words I did not have.

"Nita, you'll notice that Jesus is not hanging on your cross. The cross is empty. This symbolizes Jesus' resurrection from the dead. Now, what this means to me is that death is very painful for all of us. It's like a crucifixion. But beyond death there is another experience of life that is so wonderful we can't comprehend it.

"Nita, your daddy isn't dead. He's alive. And I hope that this cross will remind you that when death is over, there is resurrection for all of us. One of these days you and your dad and everybody that you have ever loved will be together again."

The room was silent. Gazing at the fire, I saw the prism of my own tears reflecting the intensity of the moment. And the hardest words were yet to be spoken. "Oh God," I thought, "help me say the right thing to Debbie."

Looking at Debbie, I was stunned at how young she looked. Then it hit me that she was the same age my mom was when my dad died. Momma seemed like an old lady to me then—a young teenager's perspective. But now I realized how young and vulnerable she was, how one's perspective changes over a life-time.

"Debbie," I began, struggling to think clearly, "Debbie, your cross is different than Blake's and Nita's. Sculpted on your cross is the imprint of a shepherd and three sheep. It's a shepherd's cross, and Beth and I chose this one especially for you.

"You've got a lot of shepherding to do raising these two kids. That's an awesome responsibility. But always remember that there is also a Shepherd watching over you. God will protect you and enable you in whatever you need to do. He'll give you his

strength, wisdom, love, and encouragement. He'll lead you to
green pasture and still waters. And he will restore your soul.
Debbie, you've got to believe that. And maybe this shepherd's
cross will remind you from time to time."

It was an evening I will never forget. Late that night I hugged
Debbie and the kids goodbye and drove off into a drizzling darkness. Watching the headlights guide me down the highway, I
thought about what I had said, the symbolic truth reflected in
the cross, and I was overcome with the reality of how empty and
senseless life would be if there were not a God, a Good Shepherd.
Pulling over to the side of the road, I finally let the tears go, let
the feelings pour out. I felt safe enough to cry.

As raindrops pattered the windshield, lightning flashed
across the sky and trees stepped out of darkness. With the crack
of thunder a memory was triggered and I realized that I was once
again near Swanson's Woods. Nearly thirty years had passed since
my friends and I had gotten lost hunting in those woods on that
winter night. Yet, I still felt like the same kid, running through
the darkness, praying for another glimpse of light. "Some things
never change," I thought. "We walk by faith and not by sight!"

Driving north from Fort Valley and away from tender memories, I felt a presence, an arm around me, a shepherd's staff gently touching my side. I found my lips moving, slowly uttering the
words, "Surely goodness and mercy shall follow me all the days
of my life, and I shall dwell in the house of the Lord forever."

I called Debbie several nights ago. Six months have passed, and
she is well. Human beings are amazing survivors. And she is
doing far more than surviving. Looking toward a new career, she
is reaching out toward a future that will be bright. Strength is
returning. God is with her.

And God is with you and me. None of us is protected from
pain and death, but all of us are offered the same promise of
the future. Time is moving toward an eternity of reunion with

156   all whom we have loved and who have loved us. And human
        life, even in its darkest moments, is being directed toward
        God's purpose.

        Sometimes symbols are all that we have to grasp when we
        walk toward the future. The death and resurrection of Jesus
        Christ is our most important symbol, our clearest glimpses
        beyond time and eternity. Think about it.

> *When Jesus arrived, he found that Lazarus had already
> been in the tomb four days. Martha said to Jesus, "Lord, if
> you had been here, my brother would not have died. But
> even now I know that God will give you whatever you ask
> of him." Jesus said to her, "I am the resurrection and the
> life. Those who believe in me, even though they die will live,
> and everyone who lives and believes in me will never die."*
> JOHN 11:17, 21-22, 25-26.

> *If the Spirit of him who raised Jesus from the dead dwells in
> you, he who raised Christ from the dead will give life to your
> mortal bodies also through his Spirit that dwells in you.*
> ROMANS 8:11

> *The last enemy to be destroyed is death.*
> 1 CORINTHIANS 15:26

> *Listen, I will tell you a mystery! We will not all die, but we
> will all be changed, in a moment, in the twinkling of an
> eye, at the last trumpet. . . . But thanks be to God, who
> gives us the victory through our Lord Jesus Christ.*
> I CORINTHIANS 15:51-52, 57

> *We give back, to you, O God, those whom you gave to us.
> You did not lose them when you gave them to us, and we*

do not lose them by their return to you. Your dear Son has
taught us that life is eternal and love cannot die. So death
is only an horizon, and an horizon is only the limit of our
sight. Open our eyes to see more clearly, and draw us closer
to you that we may know that we are nearer to our loved
ones, who are with you. You have told us that you are
preparing a place for us; prepare us also for that happy
place, that where you are we may also be always, O dear
Lord of life and death.[1]
WILLIAM PENN

For the Christian, death does not extinguish the light. It
puts out the lamp because the dawn has come.
ANONYMOUS

We must accept finite disappointment, but we must never
lose infinite hope.[2]
MARTIN LUTHER KING, JR.

If I find in myself a desire which no experience in this
world can satisfy, the most probable explanation is that I
was made for another world.[3]
C. S. LEWIS

Dear God, give me your vision and the grace to trust you. To know that there is good reason both to live and to die.

Lord, as I conclude this book, may your Spirit use the written word to give glimpses of truth. Shine through all of our darkness and shed light upon our way. Lead us from night to never ending day. Amen.

NOTES

Introduction

1. C. S. Lewis, as quoted in *Reader's Digest*, vol. 132, no. 789 (January 1988): 117.
2. Thomas à Kempis. *The Imitation of Christ*. Book 4, Chapter 15.
3. Alfred Noyes, "Journey by Night" in *Collected Poems (1947)*.

Chapter 1—The Power of the Universe

1. Henlee H. Barnette. *Introducing Christian Ethics*. Nashville: Broadman Press, 1961. pg. 93.
2. William Barclay. *The Gospel of John*. Vol. 1, rev. ed. Philadelphia: The Westminster Press, 1975. pgs. 132-33.
3. D. M. Dawson, as quoted in *Wesleyan Advocate* (Jan. 2, 1978): 1.
4. R. H. L. Sheppard, as quoted by Halford E. Luccock. *The Acts of the Apostles in Present-Day Preaching*. Chicago: Willett, Clark and Co., 1942. pg. 146.

Chapter 2—Wire and Tinfoil

1. Paul Tillich. *The Eternal Now*. New York: Charles Scribner and Sons, 1963.
2. Dag Hammarskjöld. *Markings*. Trans. Leif Sjoberg and W. H. Auden. New York: Alfred Knopf, 1964. pg. 45.
3. Leslie D. Weatherhead. *The Christian Agnostic*. Nashville: Abingdon Press, 1965. pg. 219.
4. Brother Lawrence. *The Practice of the Presence of God*. Old Tappan, New Jersey: Spire Books, 1958. pg. 49.
5. John Greenleaf Whittier. "The Meeting" in *Library of World Poetry*. New York: Avenel Books, 1870. pg. 287.

Chapter 3—Bruised Knuckles

1. J. W. Fanning, prayer on the 150th anniversary of First Baptist Church, Athens, Georgia.
2. Anonymous, quoted in *Pulpit Helps* (December 1987).
3. John Milton. "On His Blindness" in *The Lion Book of Christian Poetry*. Ed. Pat Alexander. Oxford: Lion Publishing, 1981. pg. 31.

Chapter 4—From the Far Side of Eternity

1. Harry Emerson Fosdick. *The Meaning of Prayer*. New York: Association Press, 1949. pg. 119.
2. Henry Wadsworth Longfellow, as quoted by Harry Emerson Fosdick. Ibid. pg. 111.
3. Clarence Jordan. *Sermon on the Mount*. Valley Forge: Judson Press, 1952. pg. 109.

Chapter 5—Horns and Buckets

1. Harry Emerson Fosdick. *The Meaning of Prayer*. New York: Association Press, 1949. pg. 121.
2. George Arthur Buttrick. *Prayer*. New York: Abingdon-Cokesbury Press, 1942. pg. 119.
3. St. Augustine. *Confessions*. Baltimore: Viking Penguin, 1961. pg. 169.
4. Paul Tournier. *A Place for You*. New York: Harper & Row, 1968. pg. 168.

Chapter 6—The Birth of Dreams 159

1. Albert Schweitzer. *Memoirs of Childhood and Youth.* New York: Henry Holt and Company, 1933. pg. 75.

2. Benjamin E. Mays, as quoted in *Reader's Digest,* vol. 132, no. 792 (April 1988): 181.

3. Søren Kierkegaard. *Journals.* 1850.

4. Frederick Buechner. *The Sacred Journey.* San Francisco: Harper & Row, 1982. pg. 102.

Chapter 7—The Cup

1. James Baldwin. *Nobody Knows My Name.* New York: Dial Press, 1961.

2. John Claypool. *Opening Blind Eyes.* Nashville: Abingdon Press, 1983. pg. 89.

3. "Prayer of an Unknown Confederate Soldier." in *The Oxford Book of Prayer.* Ed. George Appleton. Oxford: Oxford University Press, 1985. pg. 119.

Chapter 8—Dreams and Contentment

1. George Moore. *The Brook Kerith.* London: W. Heinemann Ltd., 1929.

2. Pliny the Younger. *Letters.* Trans. William Melmoth. New York: Macmillan Co., 1915. 2.15.1.

3. Kahlil Gibran. *The Wisdom of Gibran.* Ed. Joseph Sheban. New York: Bantam Books, 1966. pg. 50.

4. Edith Schaeffer. *What Is a Family?* Grand Rapids, Michigan: Raven's Ridge, 1993.

Chapter 9—Saving the Past

1. Nick Stinnett and John DeFrain. *Secrets of Strong Families.* Boston: Little, Brown and Co., 1985. pg. 4.

2. Ralph Waldo Emerson, as quoted in *Link* (December 1974): 54.

3. John Leonard, as quoted by Bernard Pierre Wolff in *Friends and Friends.*

4. Martin Buxbaum, as quoted in *Pulpit Helps* (November 1987): 29.

Chapter 10—Best Friends

1. George Eliot, source unknown.

2. Ralph Waldo Emerson. *Journals.* 1836.

3. Elbert Hubbard. *The Note Book of Elbert Hubbard.* New York: W. H. Wise, 1927.

4. Henry Adams. *The Education of Henry Adams.* New York: The Modern Library, 1931.

5. David Grayson [Ray Stannard Baker]. *Adventures in Contentment.* New York: Grosset and Dunlap, 1907. pg. 8.

6. Judith Viorst. *Necessary Losses.* New York: Simon and Schuster, 1986. pgs. 170-171, 184.

Chapter 11—Biting the Hand that Helps

1. C. S. Lewis. *The Four Loves.* New York: Harcourt Brace Jovanovich, 1960.

2. Donald W. Fry, as quoted in *Mennonite* (November 9, 1982): 548.

3. Henry Wadsworth Longfellow. "Driftwood" in *Longfellow Prose Works.* Vol. I. Boston: Houghton Mifflin, 1895.

4. William James. *The Principles of Psychology.* New York: H. Holt, 1890. chap. 22.

5. Henry David Thoreau. *Journal.* Vol. 1. Boston: Houghton Mifflin Co., 1906. February 7, 1841.

Chapter 12—Unknown Friends

1. René Descartes. *A Discourse on Method.* New York: E. P. Dutton & Co., 1912. pg. 1.

2. Thomas Bailey Aldrich. "Leaves from a Notebook" in *Ponkapog Papers* in *The Writings of Thomas Bailey Aldrich.* Vol. 9. Boston: Houghton Mifflin, 1907.

3. Henry Wadsworth Longfellow. *A Psalm of Life.* 1893. st. 7.

4. Henry Adams. *The Education of Henry Adams.* New York: The Modern Library, 1931. pg. 20.

5. Albert Schweitzer, as quoted in *Pulpit Helps* (June 1982).

160

Chapter 13—The Irony of Grace

1. James Russell Lowell. "The Vision of Sir Launfal" as quoted by Leslie Weatherhead in *A Private House of Prayer*. Nashville: Abingdon Press, 1958. pg. 140.

2. Harold Kushner. *When All You've Ever Wanted Wasn't Enough*. New York: Simon and Schuster, 1986. pgs. 188-189.

3. Brother Roger. "Make Us Servants" in *The Lion Book of Famous Prayers*. Ed. Veronica Zundel. Oxford: Lion Publishing, 1983. pg. 108.

Chapter 14—Setting the Prisoner Free

1. Paul Tournier. *A Place for You*. New York: Harper & Row, 1968. pg. 180.

2. Myron Madden. *Blessing: Giving the Gift of Power*. Nashville: Broadman Press, 1988. pg. 16.

3. Albert Schweitzer. *Memoirs of Childhood and Youth*. New York: The Macmillan Company, 1955. pgs. 67-68.

Chapter 15—Embracing the Enemy

1. C. S. Lewis. "On Forgiveness" in *The Weight of Glory*. New York: Macmillan Co., 1949. pgs. 124-125.

2. Mark Twain, as quoted in *Wesleyan Advocate* (July 7, 1975): 5.

3. John Wesley, as quoted in *Good News Broadcaster* (April 1980): 14.

4. William Blake. "To the Deists" in *Jerusalem*. New York: Holt, Rinehart and Winston, 1970. pgs. 405-407.

Chapter 16—Restoration

1. Paul Tillich. *The Essential Tillich*. Ed. F. Forrester Church. New York: Macmillan Publishing Company, 1987. pg. 201.

2. Eugene O'Neill, as quoted in *Mennonite* (January 8, 1974): 32.

3. C. S. Lewis, source unknown.

Chapter 17—The Cobbler's Nail

1. Ellen Goodman. "Country Music" in *The Washington Post* (August 1986).

2. William Barclay. *John* in *Daily Study Bible*. Vol. 1, rev. ed. Philadelphia: The Westminster Press, 1975. pg. 18.

3. W. H. Davies. "Leisure" in *Songs of Joy*. London: A. C. Fifield, 1911.

4. C. S. Lewis. *The Screwtape Letters*. Old Tappan, New Jersey: Fleming H. Revell, 1976.

Chapter 18—"When I Have Fears . . ."

1. John Keats. "When I Have Fears that I May Cease to Be" in *The Poems of John Keats*. Norwalk, Connecticut: Easton Press, 1980. pg. 163.

2. John R. Claypool, *Dialogue* [a publication of St. Luke's Episcopal Church, Birmingham, Alabama] (April 7, 1991).

3. Johann Wolfgang von Goethe. *Maxims and Reflection*.

4. Written on the grave of Winfred Holtby, novelist, 1898-1935.

5. Horace Kallen, as quoted by Harold Kushner in *When All You've Ever Wanted Wasn't Enough*. New York: Simon and Schuster, 1986. pgs. 188-189.

6. Judith Viorst. *Necessary Losses*. New York: Simon and Schuster, 1986. pg. 307

Chapter 19—Symbols

1. William Penn, as quoted in *The Oxford Book of Prayer*. Ed. George Appleton. Oxford: Oxford University Press, 1985. pg. 163.

2. Martin Luther King, Jr., as quoted in *Reader's Digest*, vol. 132, no. 789 (January 1988): 117.

3. C. S. Lewis. *Mere Christianity*. New York: Macmillan, 1952. pg. 120.